WORSHIP OF THE HEART

MeOtzar HoRav SERIES:
SELECTED WRITINGS OF RABBI JOSEPH B. SOLOVEITCHIK

The *MeOtzar HoRav* series
has been made possible
by a generous grant from
Ruth and Irwin Shapiro.

The publication of *Worship of the Heart*
has been enabled by a grant from
Helene and Moshe Talansky.

WORSHIP OF THE HEART

Essays on Jewish Prayer

by
Rabbi Joseph B. Soloveitchik

Edited by
Shalom Carmy

Published for
TORAS HORAV FOUNDATION
by KTAV Publishing House

MeOtzar HoRav Series:

Selected Writings of Rabbi Joseph B. Soloveitchik

Editorial-Publication Board:

David Shatz, Series Editor

Joel B. Wolowelsky, Associate Editor

Reuven Ziegler, Director of Archives

Volume One
Family Redeemed
Edited by David Shatz and Joel B. Wolowelsky

Volume Two
Worship of the Heart
Edited by Shalom Carmy

WORSHIP OF THE HEART
Essays on Jewish Prayer
Rabbi Joseph B. Soloveitchik
Edited by Shalom Carmy

© 2018 Toras HoRav Foundation
Second edition
This material is protected by copyright and may not be reproduced in any form, including translation, without permission in writing from the
Toras HoRav Foundation, 425 Park Avenue, Suite 970, New York, NY 10022

Library of Congress Cataloging-in-Publication Data

Soloveitchik, Joseph B.
  Worship of the heart: essays on Jewish prayer / by Joseph B. Soloveitchik; edited by Shalom Carmy.
      p. cm. (Meotzar horav; v.2)
Includes indexes
  ISBN 978-0-88125-771-7
1. Prayer – Judaism. 2. Shema. I. Carmy, Shalom. II. Title.

BM669 .S67 2002
296.4'5—dc21

2002028973

KTAV Publishing House, 527 Empire Blvd. Brooklyn, NY 11225
Website: www.ktav.com Email: orders@ktav.com
ph: (718)972-5449 / Fax: (718)972-6307
Printing year: 2018

• Table of Contents •

• Preface •

Worship of the Heart: Essays on Jewish Prayer is the second volume of the MeOtzar HoRav Series: Selected Writings of Rabbi Joseph B. Soloveitchik. Rabbi Soloveitchik zt'l (1903-1993) was not only one of the outstanding talmudists of the twentieth century, but also one of its most creative and seminal Jewish thinkers. Drawing from a vast reservoir of Jewish and general knowledge, "the Rav," as he is widely known, brought Jewish thought and law to bear on the interpretation and assessment of the modern experience. On the one hand, he built bridges between Judaism and the modern world; yet at the same time he vigorously upheld the integrity and autonomy of the Jew's faith commitment, and in particular the commitment to a life governed by Halakhah, Jewish law.

For over four decades, Rabbi Soloveitchik commuted weekly from his home in Brookline, Massachusetts to New York City, where he gave the senior *shiur* (class in Talmud) at the Rabbi Isaac Elchanan Theological Seminary (RIETS), affiliated with Yeshiva University, and, in his early years there, also taught Jewish Philosophy at the University's Bernard Revel Graduate

School. Generations of rabbinical students were taught and inspired by him—among them many of the future leaders of the Orthodox and broader Jewish community. By his extensive personal teaching and influence, as well as by serving locally as the chief rabbinic figure in Boston, where he founded the Maimonides School, he contributed vitally to the dynamic resurgence of Orthodox Judaism in America. The thousands of people who regularly flocked to his public lectures in Boston and New York in halakhic, philosophical and Biblical topics were consistently enthralled and inspired. Rabbi Soloveitchik stands, indeed, as one of the great religious leaders of our time. Even now, after his passing, his teachings—"the Rav's Torah"—are always eagerly sought, and his words continue to ring with relevance and authority.

Although many of Rabbi Soloveitchik's writings and discourses have been published over the years, much additional material, rich and evocative, remains in handwritten manuscripts. THE TORAS HORAV FOUNDATION was established by family members and former students to disseminate these and other works, with the aims of enhancing both our grasp of Rabbi Soloveitchik's philosophy and our understanding of the diverse topics he addresses. We congratulate and thank Rabbi Shalom Carmy, who began this work in concert with the Rav himself, for bringing these essays by the Rav on the topic of Jewish prayer to a long-waiting public.

Alas, it is impossible to read the Rav's powerful and challenging essays without undergoing a profound sense of the loss we have all incurred with the passing of this giant. But the reader who experiences them, who absorbs and appreciates their rare blend of intellectual sweep and energizing passion, will find them to be an invaluable, integral part of his or her own spiritual quest.

David Shatz
Joel B. Wolowelsky

❧ Introduction

A hallmark of Rabbi Soloveitchik's approach is his insistence on elucidating Judaism from within the sources of Halakhah. Prayer, with its intricate interplay of legal, liturgical and experiential motifs, provides an extraordinarily fertile demonstration of his method. While his analysis draws on many sources in the Bible, Talmud and medieval Jewish philosophy, and utilizes the insights of his general philosophical studies, this volume works from and to the prayerbook; to be precise, the *Amidah*, the reading of *Shema*, and the texts surrounding the *Shema*. We briefly describe here these fundamental building blocks of the prayer service mandated by Halakhah that are central to the book and then continue with an overview of the major themes in the Rav's philosophy of prayer and their presentation in the book.

Tefillah—prayer in the narrow sense of the term—refers to the *Amidah* (literally, the prayer recited while standing before God). The *Amidah*, popularly called *Shemoneh Esreh*, is recited three times a day. It comprises three sections: the first three benedictions consist of praise (*shevah*); the middle thirteen contain various petitions (*bakkashah*); the concluding three are devoted to thanksgiving (*hoda'ah*). On special days (Sabbath and major holidays) the middle section is replaced with a benediction pertinent to the day. On these days, and on minor holidays, an additional service (*musaf*) alludes to the distinctive nature of the day. Almost all the discussions of the *Amidah* in this book focus on the weekday service.

In the morning and evening services the *Amidah* is preceded by the recitation of *Shema*. *Shema* contains three biblical portions: Deuteronomy 6:4-9; 11:13-21; Numbers 15:37-41. Between the first verse ("Hear O Israel") and the second ("And you shall love") is interposed an adaptation of Psalm 72:19 ("Blessed be the Name of the Glory of His kingdom"). The Biblical texts are preceded by two benedictions, the first acknowledging God's creation of the natural order, the second devoted to God's love for Israel as manifested in the giving of the Torah. *Shema* is followed both morning and evening by a benediction commemorating the redemption from Egypt. The texts of these benedictions recited in the morning service (*shaharit*) and in the evening (*ma'ariv*) are different. The chapters of this book that deal with the first of the benedictions preceding the *Shema* focus on the morning version.

Let us move on to the Rav's analysis of prayer. It revolves around two poles. The first is his conviction that Halakhah is the key to Jewish religious life. Prayer and other elements of the liturgy are obligatory halakhic performances. Whether the obligation to recite a particular text is biblical or rabbinic in origin, and whether these texts are biblical or rabbinic in provenance, one must read these texts. It is important to learn from these texts too, for the prayerbook is not only the statutory articulation of our relationship to God but our training in that relationship as well.

There is no study without discrimination. The order of prayer is not an undifferentiated, unstructured series of recitations. The reading of *Shema*, with its acceptance of the yoke of God, is a very different halakhic and existential gesture than the *Amidah* prayer, in which man speaks to God about his needs. The kind of gratitude that one should feel and express at the end of the *Amidah*, standing in the Divine presence, as it were, after having addressed God about his or her needs, is not identical with the kind of gratefulness felt towards God in other situations. Studying the laws governing prayer and understanding the ideas expressed in prayer and the structure of the liturgy, are therefore essential in order to relate properly to the act of prayer. This element in the Rav's thinking about prayer is thus oriented both to practice and to intellectual penetration.

This legal and intellectual emphasis coexists with an intense emotional undercurrent. A passage from "Exaltation of God and Redeeming the Aesthetic" is typical of the consciousness found on almost every page.

The Rav writes:

> It is impossible to imagine prayer without, at the time, feeling the nearness and greatness of the Creator... We cling to Him as a living God, not as an idea, as abstract Being. We are in His company and are certain of His sympathy. There is, in prayer, an experience of emotions which can only be produced by direct contact with God.

The magnetic power of the Rav's analysis in this volume, like the fascination of his other works and his oral discourse, derives in part from his ability to move effortlessly, sometimes within the same paragraph, from the intellectually disciplined world of halakhic or literary analysis, or from a survey of relevant trends in the history of Western philosophy and religious scholarship, to the whirlpool of passionate existence.

But the Rav's yoking together of intellect and passion in his discussion of prayer is not only a product of personal profundity and rhetorical skill. It is deeply rooted in key aspects of his halakhic method and his philosophical outlook.

In his study of Halakhah, the Rav exhibited a special affinity for those *mitzvot* that can be categorized as both objective, behavioral norms and as subjective performances realized inwardly. In these cases the *ma'aseh* (performance) of the *mitzvah* is external, while the *kiyyum* (fulfillment) is inward. The kind of intention required for such *mitzvot* depends on the interaction between the objective and subjective dimensions, and it is for this reason that the Rav devotes some of the most detailed halakhic discussion in this book to the question of intention with respect to the *Amidah* (ch. 2) and to *Shema* (ch. 6).

The need for inwardness in the fulfillment of commandments like *tefillah* highlights one of the Rav's central concerns in his engagement with Western culture: the condition of man. Prayer, for the Rav, is both an expression of human nature and a reflection of human nature. The themes that the *Amidah* articulates—praise, petition based on awareness of need, thanksgiving—presuppose that these emotions are legitimate and that ordinary human beings are capable of experiencing them. Education to prayer teaches not only how to verbalize these emotions, but also how to cultivate them. The complicated philosophical line that begins in chapter 2 and dominates chapters 3 and 4 offers an account of fundamental elements in human existence like boredom, aesthetic experience, shame and ethical yearning as a means of exploring the consciousness of need accessible in ordinary life. In these chapters, and elsewhere, the Rav draws creatively upon the resources of modern Continental philosophy and phenomenology of religion, along with the ideas of medieval Jewish philosophy. But though the vocabulary and mode of discourse may seem daunting to the philosophically uninitiated, the reader who, trusting the Rav's powers of exposition, perseveres, will be rewarded with a wealth of psychological-religious insight that enriches not only his or her prayer but the totality of life.

Several additional themes characteristic of the Rav's thought surface frequently in his work on prayer. Readers should keep these ideas in mind even when they are not in the foreground of the discussion.

It is one of the Rav's oft-repeated convictions that the Halakhah is "democratic." This means that ordinary men and women are capable of living in conformity to Halakhah, and that Halakhah addresses itself to ordinary human beings. The democratic orientation of Halakhah determines the nature and scope of halakhic prayer. On the one hand, halakhic prayer is not about the cultivation of unworldly, ecstatic states of mind accessible only to mystics and other religious virtuosi. On the other hand, the halakhic liturgy is rooted in the everyday emotions and experiences that should be endemic to the human condition: praise, need, gratitude, devotion.

The primary role of petition in the *Amidah* is a corollary of this outlook. If Judaism is to bring the entire human being to God in prayer, it is essential that man come before Him with his entire being; since man has needs, his prayer must feature prominently his concern about those needs. Here the Rav, unlike some Jewish thinkers who reinterpret the halakhic highlighting of petition, vigorously contrasts Judaism with spiritual attitudes that disdain petitionary prayer.

Even while he stresses the ubiquity of need in human existence, and the consequent human need for prayer, for the opportunity to petition God respecting our needs, the Rav posits prayer as a gift rather than a right. Had God not called upon man to approach Him in prayer, we should not have presumed to do so. To borrow from the terminology of Brisker Talmudic analysis: *tefillah* requires a *mattir*—one cannot enter His presence with our requests without His granting us permission. It is for this reason that the Rav, in "Reflections on the *Amidah*," celebrates Maimonides' classification of prayer as a biblical, rather than rabbinically instituted, commandment.

It should already be clear to the reader that the Rav's mode of thinking, in particular his thoughts about prayer in all its forms, does not shirk confrontation with the difficulties and paradoxes of human existence. This ruthless honesty also finds expression in his blunt avowal of the fact that man, on occasion, feels distant and estranged from God; God may be experienced as absent, even as hostile. This aspect of religious existence is most fully explored in "The Absence of God and the Community of Prayer," where, for example, the Rav does not hesitate to state that

> The religious experience not only warms, but also chills with horror. The religious is not only swayed by joy, but also by sadness and pain. All the modern theories about the healing function of religion see only one phase of the religious experience, the sublimated one.

When he reviewed this section of the manuscript with me, the Rav commented that this truth, however familiar to the student of classical Jewish sources—he mentioned Lamentations, Job and the Psalms specifically—is a hard one, a shocking one, for many modern people to accept. Not the least of the Rav's virtues was his willingness to acknowledge and to utter hard truths. Not his least strength as a teacher of Judaism, is that he comprehended the sadness and the pain within the broader framework of Jewish existence and human existence. His canon included Lamentations and Job, but also the great hymns of "*Borkhi nafshi,* Let my soul bless the Lord" (Psalms 103-104) and the *vita activa* (active life) of unceasing Torah study, unstinting ethical dedication and meticulous *mitzvah* performance. To be exposed to his work in all its variety is to know the "sober joy" and Jamesian "solemnity" that he ascribed to halakhic man in his essay with that title.

• • •

The following summaries are meant to convey the structure and direction of the argument before us, and to clarify some points that might baffle the reader uninitiated in the Rav's mode of thought, or lacking adequate background in the classical Jewish disciplines or the Western philosophical and religious literature. It goes without saying that they cannot serve as a substitute for an encounter with the Rav's nuanced discussion.

Prayer and the Media of Religious Experience

Chapters 1-5 are best read consecutively, as a unified presentation. "Prayer and the Media of Religious Experience" places prayer within the larger context of Divine-human communication. Prayer is not the only such medium, to the exclusion of other media. Prayer is part of a life in which human beings also worship God through their intellectual engagement with Him, through the emotional quest, and by directing their will to His service. In arguing for the intellectual love of God, the Rav draws on the philosophy of Maimonides and on the halakhic precept of Torah study as it has been interpreted by Jewish thinkers.

For his account of the emotional quest, he utilizes R. Judah Halevi's *Kuzari* together with Maimonides. While the *Kuzari* passage he adduces deals with classical prophecy, the Rav stresses that his words are not irrelevant to our situation: "although *nevu'ah* (prophecy) has come to an end, the immediate apprehension of God has not been eliminated from the perspective of our religious experience." This impulse to seek contemporary existential equivalents for the extraordinary phenomena presented in the Bible is characteristic of the Rav's thinking; it is a consequence of his practical-halakhic tendency, for which the Divine discourse of Scripture must always have something to say to the human condition.

If Halakhah champions the intellectual and emotional approaches to God, as the Rav points out, most certainly it is oriented to the volitional mode—the service of God in action. Having introduced the reader to these three modes of worship, all of which stand in an important relationship to prayer without being identical with it, the Rav outlines the fourth medium, the dialogical, and briefly sketches the themes of man's conversation with God, praise, gratitude and most prominently, petition. This section contains illustrations from the holiday *Amidah* and from the benedictions of the marriage service.

Prayer, Petition and Crisis

"Prayer, Petition and Crisis" opens with a discussion of the relationship between objective and subjective aspects of certain *mitzvot*. There are commandments of the hand and commandments of the heart, and the latter too are connected to norms of external behavior. This principle, which we adumbrated above, entails that experiential norms are anchored in the external realization of concrete actions. This is needed because, as the Rav observes, "Halakhah is distrustful of the genuineness and depth of our inner life, because of its vagueness, transience and volatility." This argument is embedded in a halakhic analysis that centers on Maimonides' definition of the commandment of *avodah she-ba-lev* (worship of the heart). The Rav's goal is to demonstrate that unlike standard actional *mitzvot*, which can be fulfilled without *kavvanah* (intention) or with a minimal kind of intention, prayer must be accompanied by *kavvanah*. As there is technique in painting, which enables the artist's personal vision to find expression, so the normative physical performances required in prayer support the intimate personal experience.

Drawing on Maimonides' *Guide*, the Rav defines the passional experience that ought to be part of prayer. In its ideal form, what is spoken of is nothing less than an all-consuming, perpetual consciousness of the Divine. But this description is suited to the extraordinary individual. Hence the Rav is brought up against the "democratic" problem: how can genuine prayer be a live option for the ordinary person? The Rav's answer to this question determines the next several chapters of the book. In brief, he maintains that the content of statutory prayer, praise, gratitude and most of all petition, addresses universal aspects of the human condition. Not every nuance of spiritual existence is available to everyone. But those elements that Halakhah formulates as part of prayer are accessible to ordinary human beings.

The common denominator of the basic themes in the *Amidah* is that they articulate a consciousness of *tzarah* (distress). The human condition is characterized by vulnerability and need. Prayer emerging *de profundis*, from out of the depths, thus expresses the everyday concerns of human beings. This fundamental connection between distress and prayer the Rav discovers in Nahmanides' teaching that the prayer that is biblically mandated is that offered in time of distress. While it is not part of his definition of prayer, Maimonides too speaks of the obligation to pray when in distress.

The Rav now postulates two types of distress. One is obvious but superficial—when, for example, an external calamity befalls a person. Such conventional suffering usually has a public nature: illness, poverty or death. Contrasting to this is the depth crisis, which does not befall the sufferer from the outside but reflects a certain kind of self-awareness: "The crisis is encountered in the strangeness of human destiny, of which man is not aware at all unless he is willing to acquaint himself with it." For the individual who is willing to become aware of his or her distress prayer is always meaningful. One never achieves a point of total satisfaction and security. And thus the Rav concludes, "I believe that even the simplest man may perceive and comprehend this existential tragic aspect of man."

The Human Condition and Prayer

"The Human Condition and Prayer" explores different elements in the experience of depth crisis. Underlying much of the analysis is the crucial conflict between two existential tendencies: the desire and need for permanence and uniformity, on the one hand, and the appetite for change and novelty, on the other hand. The Rav traces these two orientations all the way back to the Greek pre-Socratic philosophers Parmenides and Heraclitus, the former asserting the unity of being and denying the reality of change, the latter insisting on the pervasiveness of flux. For the Rav, their respective views represent not merely a disagreement about the nature of being, but a tension between different ways of experiencing the world and perceiving value in it. The Rav believes that the Heraclitean tendency has triumphed, both emotionally and ontologically. Hence human beings are dissatisfied with unchanging, repetitive patterns, and are restlessly in search of an alternative to their situations.

The first phenomenon the Rav mentions is boredom, which reflects man's lack of ease when confined to his or her present state, however delightful it may have seemed only yesterday. This Heraclitean impulse for change is opposed by the permanence posited by the cognitive gesture and the ethical imperative. The desire for truth, and the manner in which truth is sought, places a value on permanence and persevering. Likewise, the ethical law is binding all the time, and does not take into account the monotonous quality of this commitment. Against these essential manifestations of a Parmenidean awareness the Rav sets the aesthetic type. The word *aesthesis* in Greek refers to sensual experience, and continued to have that meaning in European philosophy until the end of the 18th century, from which time on, it refers primarily to the experience of beauty or the artistic. The Rav connects the more recent sense of the word with the older one: a life devoted to beauty is a life oriented to the tangible, to particular, mutable perception, rather than to the general and abstract. The aesthetic is consequently without any purpose outside itself. Intellectual and ethical activity, by contrast, are purposeful (teleological) and aim at goals (truth, usefulness, goodness and so forth) that transcend and go beyond the activity itself. Because all three of these impulses are essential to the existence of man, the Rav therefore concludes that "the theoretician and ethicist in him [man] are at war with the aesthete."

In a further analysis of the aesthetic, the Rav analyzes the interpretation of original sin in Maimonides' *Guide*. In the Rav's reading of Maimonides, sin is the aesthetic orientation overriding the ethical imperative. This section of the essay contains many fascinating insights regarding the difference between moral shame (when one acts wrongly) and aesthetic shame (e.g. when one is observed in the nude), and the difference between shame and embarrassment. The central point, however, is that the sinful triumph of the aesthetic over the ethical must inevitably result in boredom, insofar as the aesthetic in itself is without purpose or permanence. It would, of course, be unfortunate if the aesthetic experience were indeed sinful and destructive. In that case an essential dimension of human existence would be purposeless and unredeemed. The essay ends with an unresolved question: Can the aesthetic awareness be properly integrated and redeemed?

Exaltation of God and Redeeming the Aesthetic

"Exaltation of God and Redeeming the Aesthetic" takes up this question. The Rav argues that aesthetic, immediate experience can be redeemed if it is brought into relation with something beyond it. In this way the aesthetic transcends itself and become teleologic, just as the cognitive or moral orientations reach out to something beyond them. When the aesthetic becomes critical of itself and seeks some value beyond itself, its affinity to religious emotion becomes marked.

In bridging the gap between the aesthetic and the religious, the experience of exaltedness is of great importance. The sense of beauty may be ennobling, but it does not inherently suggest to man "the vision of something unique and great that is connected to witnessing the beautiful." This element of transcendence points to the religious apprehension of the Divine. Thus the aesthetic experience of the exalted forces the aesthete to transcend the merely immediate quality of his experience. By criticizing the immediacy and lack of purposiveness in the aesthetic, the exalted discovers the common ground between aesthetics and religion.

The above philosophical analysis is accompanied by discussions of several pertinent Biblical passages. These include Isaiah's exalted vision of God's throne (Isaiah 6) and the aesthetic enjoyment that is part and parcel of the religious experience celebrated in Psalms 19 and 104. Working from this position, the Rav elaborates on the sensual, even erotic imagery often found in the Bible's depiction of religious experience. He bases this thesis on statements in R. Judah Halevi's *Kuzari* and on the evidence of Deuteronomy 5, Psalm 34 and the Song of Songs, among other sources. He insists that this imagery is particularly important because it precludes our thinking of God in purely abstract terms. Such abstraction would make the dialogue of prayer impossible: "Community existence is only possible if both parties joining into this type of fellowship encounter each other as real personalities whose presence is immediately felt and acknowledged." The Rav here, and elsewhere, emphasizes the vividness of religious life. Although he stresses that sensuous imagery need not be pictorial imagery, his lack of embarrassment, *pace* Maimonides, in considering the prevalence of such imagery may be surprising to rationalistic readers. Despite his stress on the vividness of religious experience, the Rav contrasts the hymns characteristic of "civilized religion" with the wild behavior found in "primitive religion." In oral discourse, the Rav observed that religious ceremonial employing choreography and instrumentation, is strictly limited by Halakhah. This is because the emotions unleashed in these activities, more than in verbal performance, threaten to over-power the logos.

This survey of the emotional range represented in the Biblical accounts of human religious experience leads to a consideration of hymnal praise. The Rav believes that the rapture of praise and thanksgiving requires the aesthetic perception of beauty. He examines several expressions of praise in the Bible and in Halakhah (i.e. benedictions recited as a response to certain phenomena). The Rav stresses that the religious experience is fascinating and attractive, and at the same time frightening, forbidding, alien and crushing. The Rav's citation of Psalm 2:11, "Serve God in fear; rejoice in trembling" captures the gist of this insight. He borrows the term "numinous" as a description of this overwhelming, awesome strangeness from the early 20th century Protestant thinker Rudolf Otto.

The last part of the chapter is devoted to the pair of Psalms (103-104) beginning with the phrase *"Borkhi nafshi,* Let my soul bless the Lord." The first exemplifies thanksgiving; the second, praise. Overall the Rav's explication reinforces the themes sketched above: that God is experienced in the majestic beauty of the creation; that man's encounter with the majestic is tied to a sense of his own worthlessness; that God is ultimately unknowable. To get the fine detail of the discussion it is necessary to read the text carefully, preferably with Bible in hand. In this section the Rav also introduces the distinction between two different moments in religious life, both of which arouse a sense of God's awesomeness: the experience of Divine presence and the experience of His absence, the hiding of His Face.

The Absence of God and the Community of Prayer

"The Absence of God and the Community of Prayer" continues where the previous chapter leaves off. Judaism maintains that man encounters God in the world of nature and in the message (*kerygma*) of history. The absence of God is experienced in both realms: In nature, "the numinous is apprehended in the seemingly mechanical arrangement of cosmic occurrence." This feeling has become more intense in modern times, with the triumph of mechanistic causal explanation and the reign of the machine. "[I]n the historical realm the numinous comes to expression when man suddenly becomes aware of the unreasonableness of historical occurrence." The prophets, Habakkuk in particular, though never wavering in their faith, shuddered before the terror of Divine absence, the indifference of the cosmos and the historical realm. Unlike Greek tragedy, however, Judaism recognizes these moments as part of a larger story culminating in redemption.

Redemption, for the Rav, should not be identified simplistically with external events that benefit the individual or the group. It is predicated on the formation of community with God. The overcoming of Divine absence is thus the overcoming of man's metaphysical loneliness. In the later sections of the essay, the Rav distinguishes the depth-crisis of loneliness from boredom. Boredom results from lack of purpose; loneliness is a lack of roots, a sense of estrangement. "Through prayer, writes the Rav, "man accomplishes the impossible: the transformation of the numinous into the kerygamatic, fear into love and absence into presence."

The impossibility to which the Rav refers is, of course, conceptual. The achievement of community out of lack of community is inexplicable. But as is often the case in the Rav's thought, what is inconceivable, and appears at first glance to be impossible, can be accomplished by entering into the appropriate intellectual and existential orientation. This part of the book ends by outlining several "methods" by which the prayer community comes into being. One element that facilitates prayer is identification with the paradigmatic figures of the Bible, and with the model of dialogue with God presented in Scripture. It is not accidental that the *Amidah* begins by referring to the "God of Abraham, God of Isaac and God of Jacob." A second element is the realization that God relates Himself to man not only in the order of creation, where one apprehends His majesty, but also in revelation, in the Torah. The encounter with God through revelation engenders moral demands addressed to man; in this respect Judaism differs from what the Rav calls "subjectivist religion." Because human beings can share in the moral law, they can seek to attain community with God through imitating His ways.

Intention (Kavvanah) in Reading Shema and in Prayer

"Intention (*Kavvanah*) in Reading *Shema* and in Prayer" is the first of the four essays on *Shema*. Following the opening section, which recapitulates the opening of ch. 2, the Rav addresses the question of *kavvanah* for *Shema*. As the halakhic question is not explicitly discussed in the Talmud, the Rav here engages in the most complex halakhic analysis in the book. In summary, he maintains that in reciting *Shema*, as in *tefillah*, a specific intention is halakhically required, over and beyond a general intention to perform the *mitzvah*. The Rav ascribes the formulation of this idea to the 14th century Spanish authority R. Shlomo ben Adret (Rashba) although he demonstrates that this idea is already implicit in Maimonides' halakhic and philosophical works.

The Rav next proceeds to define the fundamental intention of *Shema* as "accepting the yoke of the kingdom of Heaven." *Tefillah* requires man to stand in the presence of God and to address Him in the second person, while in *Shema* the individual is not speaking to God. *Shema* takes "the form of declaration, confession, profession of faith." *Shema*, therefore, is less of a personal encounter, and more of an intellectual commitment. "In *Shema* one assents to and accepts authority." Detailed halakhic comparison of the laws governing *tefillah* with those pertinent to reciting *Shema* confirms this thesis. These laws include questions about posture, state of mind, and permissibility of interruption during the respective performances.

The lecture concludes with some salient remarks on method in the investigation of Jewish thought. The Rav's major concern here is the proper integration of halakhic data, which he regards as central, with that of Aggadah and, in the case of prayer, with the study of the liturgy itself. He exemplifies the last point by proposing that the three benedictions preceding and following the *Shema* elucidate the three biblical portions that comprise it.

The Essence of Shema: Unity of God, Love of God and the Study of His Law

"The Essence of *Shema*: Unity of God, Love of God and the Study of His Law" begins with a halakhic analysis the goal of which is to locate precisely, within the first portion recited, the verses that contain the gist of *Shema*. From a detailed consideration of Maimonides' utilization of his Talmudic sources, the Rav infers three essential themes: unity of God; love of God; study of Torah.

The discussion of unity proceeds by analyzing the aggadic treatment of the phrase *Barukh shem kevod malkhuto* that is recited after the opening verse. The story about Jacob speaking this refrain to his sons implies that the commitment to Divine unity is manifested in self-identification with Jewish religious history. It also implies that the conception of Divine unity goes back before revelation, to the period of the Patriarchs.

Regarding the content of Divine unity, the Rav stresses that Jewish thought prefers to work "inductively," from particular points of departure instead of starting with abstract foundations. Therefore he regards the practical halakhic articulations of Divine unity as more fruitful sources of insight than purely metaphysical argumentation. This is demonstrated through a comparison of Maimonides' formulations of Divine unity in his

Sefer ha-Mitzvot (Book of Commandments) and in the *Mishneh Torah*. From here he arrives at the halakhic principle that acknowledging the unity of God is not only an intellectual act but is also expressed in the willingness to suffer and to die for this confession of faith. The chapter ends by contrasting this integration of ethical commitment and doctrinal assertion with the Greek philosophical outlook according to which ethics are primarily a means to the intellectual life.

Immanence and Transcendence: Comments on Birkat Yotzer Or

The next chapter, "Immanence and Transcendence: Comments on *Birkat Yotzer Or* (Who creates light)," returns to the first of the introductory benedictions. *Yotzer Or*, whose content is God's sovereignty over nature, corresponds to the first biblical portion of *Shema*, that is to say, it focuses on the unity of God. The principle here is that Divine unity implies the unity of God's cosmic governance with His moral providence. The first part of the essay elucidates the Jewish concept of creation, according to which the world is substantially separate from God, yet does not have a separate existence apart from Him, carefully distinguishing it from the pantheistic view of Spinoza, according to which God is the only substance, or the doctrine of emanation in Plotinus which, the Rav holds, makes God more of a principle than a reality.

The second part of the essay demonstrates the unity of the moral will and the cosmic order in this benediction. The Rav explores the opening phrase of the benediction in the light of its biblical source in Isaiah, showing that the text refers to the challenge of integrating evil in God's all-benevolent creation. He then goes on to examine the angelic song included in the blessing. Disagreeing with academic scholars who claimed that this passage does not fit the context, the Rav argues that the angelic service of this blessing is juxtaposed with the manifestation of

Divine will in the cosmic order so as to indicate the ultimate unity of the two—nature driven by mechanical law; the angels, by love and awe. (The scholarly position which the Rav rejects can be found in Ismar Elbogen, *Der Jüdische Gottesdienst*, section 9.)

Accepting the Yoke of Heaven

"Accepting the Yoke of Heaven" returns to the themes of chapter 7, while presupposing chapter 8, in particular the idea that man is separate from God and at the same time at one with Him. The opening section probes, both philosophically and metaphorically (comparing the relation of man and God to that between infant and mother) the nature of this love and identification. This is followed by a reworking of the medieval notion, according to which the motion of the planets is driven by a quest for the Divine: obsolete as physics, this idea nevertheless captures a spiritual principle that appeals to the Rav. Because, in a sense, all nature seeks after God, it is possible for man to sanctify the full range of human activities, including those that are biological in origin. Thus the essay arrives at a conclusion about man's natural functions that parallels that of chapter 7 dealing with intellectual activity.

Reflections on the Amidah

"Reflections on the *Amidah*" is the longest chapter, and the only one that the Rav published (in the original Hebrew) while he was alive. The opening sections are dominated by the idea that man is able to approach God in *tefillah* only because God has told us to do so. "Had the Torah not commanded prayer as the singular medium of expression for inward worship," writes the Rav, we do not know what the God-seeking human being, whose soul thirsts for the living God, would do." Maimonides was the first of the major medieval authorities to rule that *tefillah* is biblically commanded. The Rav celebrates this ruling as one that redeems from muteness much of our religious experience.

Next the Rav describes the threefold structure of the *Amidah*, the precedents for traditional prayer in the lives of the Patriarchs and the sacrificial cult, and the means by which the Halakhah justifies the endeavor of petitionary prayer. This is followed by a meditation on the first three benedictions, the praise that is prologue to the petition. In the Rav's reading, these three benedictions articulate a dialectical experience of prayer. The initial approach, in the first one (*Avot*), right after the prefatory request that God open our lips, is via the awareness of *hesed* (Divine graciousness) and via the community of the Patriarchs. The second (*Gevurot*) represents man's weakness when overwhelmed by God's mightiness, an unlimited power that is manifest in God's providential acts, most notably the resurrection of the dead. The third (*Kedushah*) recognizes God as awesome.

In order to explicate the experiential possibility of prayer in the light of these three benedictions, the Rav expounds the fundamental idea of prayer as sacrifice. In prayer, confronting the awesomeness of the Divine, man responds by surrendering himself. If the ritual of animal sacrifice has been suspended due to the destruction of the Temple, the experience of human sacrifice remains very much alive. If in the first benediction man approaches God confident and optimistic, and in the second he stands before Him frail and helpless, then the third "commands both the human being who believes in his value and importance and the human being who negates himself, to offer up their entire being to God."

In this connection the Rav comments further on the sacrificial element. Judaism rejects the division of the world into the sacred, in which man propitiates God, and the secular, to which God has no claim. Where such division exists, prayer and sacrifice become hypocritical, as the prophets frequently preached. Surrender to God permeates all activity, but does not render worldly activity null: "Sacrifice is not identical with annihilation. The Torah was interested in life and repelled by death. The altar is not built at man's grave but at his cradle."

The central portion of the *Amidah* is petitionary, and the Rav presents and expands themes discussed earlier in the book. It is followed by the culminating thanksgiving benedictions. The Rav remarks on the mixture of thanksgiving and petition in these last three benedictions, and ties the quality of this part of the *Amidah* to the crucial dimension of sacrifice introduced earlier in the *tefillah*. In effect, the prayer reaches a double climax in the last petitionary benediction, *Shema Kolenu* ("Hear our voice") which brings to a close the requests connected to everyday human needs, and in the first thanksgiving benediction, *Retzeh* ("Accept willingly") which entreats God to accept our sacrifice. Lastly, the Rav offers the insight that the last three benedictions correspond chiastically to the first three, so that the last benediction *Sim Shalom* ("Grant peace") harks back to the confident opening of *Avot*. An essay, and a book, that again and again compels the reader to plunge into the crises of human existence ends, like the *Amidah* itself, in a moment of peace, serenity and light.

• • •

The general theory of prayer in chapters 1-5 is taken primarily from a series of notebooks labelled "*Seder ha-Tefillot* (Order of Prayer)," composed in 1956-7 as the basis for a course at Yeshiva University's Bernard Revel Graduate School. A general lecture on prayer, delivered to the Rabbinical Council of America in 1959, covers some of the themes of the opening chapter; sections of the lecture were combined with chapters 1-2. The text also contains additional comments by the Rav when he first began to review the text for publication, and incorporates loose pages attached to the notebooks. Chapters 6-9, dealing with the liturgy of *Shema*, represent another series of note-books, entitled "Fundamentals of Prayer," from the same peri-od. I determined the order of the chapters in this volume and added chapter subheadings. Chapter 10, "Reflections on the *Amidah*," was translated by myself for this volume from the first Hebrew edition of *Ra'ayonot al ha-Tefillah*, published in 1978 in *Hadarom*. Dr. David Shatz read the translation meticu-lously and made many valuable suggestions.

I can testify from experience that the Rav was a perfectionist when it came to revising his writing for publication. Unfortunately we do not know how the Rav would have expand-ed these notebooks, what elaborations, additions, restructuring and reformulation the material would have undergone before he was satisfied that it was ready for release into the world. His for-mulations in this book do not come close to exhausting the trea-sure of insight and interpretation he amassed during a long life-time of prayer, study and teaching. Often he alludes in passing to ideas that are fully and richly worked out in other lectures and papers, some available in Hebrew, some yet unpublished. In further volumes of this series I hope, with God's help, to acquaint readers with more of the Rav's teachings on prayer in general, and on the many texts and textures of Jewish worship.

One of the quiet pleasures in completing a project of this nature is the opportunity to thank those who have helped it along the way. First, of course, is my revered teacher Rabbi Soloveitchik *zt"l* himself, who entrusted me with most of the material in the volume, commented on some of it, and was exceedingly generous with his valuable time. I am most grate-ful to Dr. Atarah Twersky for her guidance and patience throughout the editorial process. She reviewed parts of the manuscript at various times, and carefully commented on the final version in its entirety. Regrettably, Rabbi Yitzhak Twersky *zt"l* did not have the opportunity to accompany the work through its various stages; the title of the book was his sugges-tion. (The word *"avodah"* can be rendered as either "service" or "worship," and in the translation I have chosen the word that fit best in the context.) My revered teachers Rabbi Walter Wurzburger *zt"l* and Rabbi Aharon Lichtenstein were always ready to help.

I am deeply indebted to the Toras HoRav Foundation for making the Rav's writings available. David Shatz and Joel Wolowelsky were, as usual, models of collegiality, intellectual integrity and practical wisdom. Reuven Ziegler provided the manuscript of chapters 8-9 from the MeOtzar HoRav Archives at Yeshivat Har Etzion, supervised a great deal of technical work, and contributed valuable comments. David Feinberg, Avi Helfand, Rachel Leiser Levy, Alex Mondrow, Moshe Pack, Gavriel Posner, and Elie Weissman helped decipher the Rav's handwriting, checked sources and otherwise assisted. Lastly, at the risk of omitting names that deserve mention, let me note some of the individuals who have contributed to my under-standing of the texts and ideas discussed in this book and, hope-fully, in its sequels: Benjamin Balint, Michael S. Berger, Yitzchak Blau, Asher Friedman, David Gottlieb, Mark Gottlieb, Aaron Liebman, Bernard Stahl, Jerry Zeitchik. Meira Gross and Shifra Schapiro served as copy editors. Samuel Groner pre-pared the indexes. May they, and others in our community, enjoy the privilege of making the Rav's teaching their own and transmitting it to others.

Shalom Carmy

❧ "When I Speak about the Philosophy of Prayer"

Before we turn our thoughts to the analytical process of comprehension, I want to make the following reservation. John Henry Newman, at the beginning of chapter 10 of his *Essay in Aid of a Grammar of Assent,* says that in the provinces of religious inquiry, egotism is true modesty. One can express only his own feelings. He cannot and should not lay down universal postulates and general rules. He may hope that by formulating his own experiences in clear language, others may benefit from this self-revelation and enrich their own religious life. However the latter, being the most subjective and intimate of all modes of existence, is many a time inseparable from the individual personality—its character, temper, moods, and susceptibilities. Any attempt at standardization or generalization is based upon the assumption that what satisfies me is likely to please others as well. Yet, at times, my feelings and convictions are exclusively my own and I have no way to pass them on to others.

Therefore, when I speak about the philosophy of prayer or *Shema,* I do not claim universal validity for my conclusions. I am not lecturing on philosophy of prayer as such, but on prayer as understood, experienced and enjoyed by an individual. I acquaint you with my own personal experience. Whether, taking into consideration the differences between minds and the peculiarities of the individual, my experience can be detached from my idiosyncrasies and transferred to others, I do not know.

The pride and audacity which usually mark the philosophical pronouncements in the field of Jewish religion by secular scholars who have never had the opportunity to live through great religious experiences must be done away with. I am lecturing on prayer as understood, experienced and enjoyed by an individual. Of course, I try to corroborate my own convictions and feelings by coordinating them with the great disciplines of Halakhah and Aggadah. However, to say that my feeling of certitude carries universal significance would be sheer ignorance. Hence, in all humility I warn you not to ascribe to my remarks more veracity than an individual may claim for his subjective experiences.

❧ *Prayer and the Media of Religious Experience*

P rayer (*Tefillah*) is one of the media through which man communicates with the Almighty God. I purposely say "one of the media" in order to refute the doctrine advanced by the mystics, and accepted by the advocates of religious subjectivism, that prayer is the only means leading to the successful realization of our blind intent of reaching out to Him. Judaism has not subscribed to the idea of the centrality of prayer, even though it has not underestimated the importance of prayer as regards our God-searching and God-pursuing. Basically prayer is a mode of expression or objectification of our inner experience, of a state of mind, of a subjective religious act, of the adventurous and bold attempt of self-transcendence on the part of the human being, and of his incessant drive toward the infinite and eternal. This truth was discovered by Maimonides (*Hilkhot Tefillah* 1:1), when he raised the precept of prayer to the status of a Pentateuchal commandment, and rehabilitated the midrashic-aggadic term *avodah she-ba-lev* (worship of the heart).

Prayer designates certain aspects of *avodah she-ba-lev,* the intimate and silent worship of God by the heart. Worship of the heart actually embraces the total commitment of man to his Creator, his being rooted in, close to and at the same time infinitely far from God, his fear and his love of God, his anxiety and security, despair and hope, his certainty and doubts, his awareness of Being and non-being, of rationality and purposiveness, and, simultaneously, of the absurdity and meaninglessness of the human performance. Prayer is one aspect of *avodah she-ba-lev,* but worship is not confined in its process of objectification to prayer; worship expresses itself in a variety of ways, since it is the sum total of man's relationship to God. In other words, it is the quintessence of Judaism. If we want to understand *tefillah* (prayer), we must explore the media through which the religious experience manifests itself.

We shall discuss four such media of experience—the intellectual, the emotional, the volitional, and the dialogical.

The Intellectual Medium

Man must serve God at the intellectual level. Judaism believes that human thinking is only a reflex of the infinite mind and that knowledge and cognition are basically Divine possessions. Man is only allowed to share these treasures with their real Master—with God. Thought is the link connecting finite and infinite, creature and Creator. In the intellectual gesture, man meets God, and joins Him. Maimonides considers this thesis the crux of his religious philosophy. The intellectual approach to God is closely bound up either with scientific-metaphysical research and knowledge or with the study of the Torah. Maimonides considered both of these cognitive performances to be an expression of man's clinging to God. Thinking in terms of eternal truths, whether theoretical or ethical, is an act of love, of craving for God. In theory and ethos we give ourselves to Him. He claims us and our total being. God reveals Himself in the cosmic, as well as in the moral law. By discovering these principles, we meet God. In the intellectual gesture, there is an inward turning towards God, a silent communication, a speechless dialogue with the Creator, Artist and Lover. Man and God are united through the bond of wisdom (see *Mishneh Torah*, *Hilkhot Teshuvah* 10:6).

In an excerpt from Maimonides' *Guide*, which we shall discuss below, the exclusively intellectual feature in the communication between God and man is stressed with almost unrestrained zeal. The true worship of God is possible only when correct ideas of Him have previously been conceived. It is when one has arrived by way of intellectual research at a knowledge of God and His works that one commences devotion to Him; it is then that one may try to approach Him and strengthen even further the intellect which is the link to Him.

At this intellectual level, Judaism considered the study of Torah as the most sublime kind of worship, a way of meeting God, of breaking through the barrier separating the Absolute from the contingent and relative. Human intellectual engagement in the exploration of God's word, thought and law is a great religious experience, an activity bordering on the miraculous, a paradoxical bridge spanning the chasm that separates the world of vanity from infinity. The leaders of both Hasidut and Lithuanian halakhic rationalism saw in the preoccupation of the intellect with the Torah a sort of identification with Divine thought, the realization of man's longing for companionship with God, reaching the dimensions of the supra-natural *unio mystica*.

The Emotional Medium

Man is also able to approach God through his great and passionate love for Him, through an ecstatic experience which enables the finite being to transcend the bounds of finitude and to rise above the limited and relative to the heights of absoluteness and endlessness. Man, many Jewish philosophers and mystics maintained, may reach God not only through the intellect but also through the "heart," through a pure and serene state of mind, however naive and simple; through a passionate, sincere, though not intellectually enlightened love; through craving for God, even when the heart which craves has not been illumined by Divine knowledge and wisdom; in loneliness and despair, even if the lonely and despairing soul cannot interpret its own misery; or through joy and jubilation, notwithstanding the fact that the heart which is filled with gratitude and happiness is too ignorant to analyze its aroused emotions. One may find access to God in ignorance and intellectual want as long as he is truthful and his feelings are sincere and genuine.

Yehudah Halevi expounds his theory of religious emotionality in the *Kuzari*. The king of the Khazars inquires of the *haver* (Jewish spokesman) concerning the relevance of the visionary experience: "When His divinity penetrates the mind, and His unity and power and wisdom, and that all is dependent on Him, while He does not depend on anything, should not the fear of God and His love penetrate, so that we would not require these corporeal images?" (*Kuzari* 4:4). The *haver* answers him as follows:

> This is the philosophers' argument. But experience of the human soul shows that it fears when it experiences frightening sensations, and not when one is simply told about something, that it loves a beautiful form that is present, which it does not love when told about it. Do not believe the clever person who says that his thought attaches itself in an orderly manner, so that he attains what is requisite to knowing God through his intellect alone without relying on sensation... Do you not see that you cannot arrange all your prayers in thought alone without speech? (4:5)

Of course, Yehudah Halevi is speaking of prophetic vision in contrast to philosophic abstraction. Let us not forget, however, that although *nevu'ah* (prophecy) has come to an end, the immediate apprehension of God has not been eliminated from the perspective of our religious experience. The emotional approach to God via the ecstatic leap into the beyond is to be considered a direct beholding of Him. There is no need for additional visionary perceptions characteristic of prophecy. The feeling of His presence, companionship and closeness is vivid and overpowering. One feels the breath of infinity in the stillness of a clear starlit night, when he simply perceives the great miracle of being in touch with the Creator who resides beyond the endless spaces of the flying nebulae. One may feel the "unseen reality," as William James calls it, in the happiness of self-fulfillment, in the embrace of a child and in the joy of spiritual accomplishment. It is not the physical law or the mathematical formula, but the overpowering thirst for God, the great hope for and experience of Him. The craving for closeness to Being as such, with the origin and root of everything, is an *avodah she-ba-lev*. *Avodah she-ba-lev* is realized in the misery of humiliation, when the soul cries out "My God, my God, why hast Thou forsaken me" (Ps. 22:2), in the bliss of beholding His glory, when man sings out: "Raise O gates your heads... and let enter the King of glory" (Ps. 24:7), in the suffering of the human being when he wears himself out in trying to appease a desire that is renewed with every gratification, in his frustrating undertaking to lend meaning and sense to his life, in his despair over the emptiness and absurdity of existence which he, together with the wise king, recognizes as the vanity of all things. And, it is realized when he feels unburdened and happy with his destiny and accomplishments, when his life is suddenly filled with positive significance and he experiences boundless joy in existing. In a word, the emotional life of man is an outstanding medium of communication with God.

The Halakhah recognizes the legitimate role of the affective approach to God, since it formulates norms with respect to the feelings of man. The prime task of these norms is to lend religious significance to human emotion, which, on its own, is quite often devoid of rationale and comparative coherence, logical continuity and sensibility. Rabbinic passages pertaining to the love and fear of God give uncontrovertible proof of the Halakhah's concern with the sentiments of man.

Even Maimonides, the great rationalist, who considered the intellectual connection to God as the prime objective of man's pursuits and cognitive attainments, as the safest way leading to God, admitted that a rational, intellectual approach is not enough. The intellectual quest must express itself in an act of love whereby man attaches himself to the Infinite. The distinction between Maimonides and Halevi is to be understood in terms of philosophical order rather than of essence. Maimonides posits the intellect as the point of departure for the dramatic ascent of man to God that coincides with the great, passionate love of man: "according to the knowledge, so is the love" (*Hilkhot Teshuvah* 10:6). Yehudah Halevi, as an adherent of visionary experience, starts out with the emotional response of man to the vision of God to man; he depicts man confronted with the reality of the Infinite and from there he proceeds to the interpretation of the emotional experience in rational terms. Medieval Jewish philosophers who had, in the main, a good halakhic training, and were thus perpetually occupied with difficult intellectual matters, could not, like Christian mystics, simply abandon themselves to fantasies and emotional, uncontrolled outbursts and upheavals. The ecstatic moment in the religious experience must be harnessed by intellectual categories and must never exceed the bounds of rationality. Judaism has always tried to maintain a fundamental equilibrium of thought and emotion, of cognition and feeling. Feeling is always seen as a conative experience and this aspect is analyzed in the light of rational criteria. The meaning is analyzed, the worth of the striving is examined, and the possibilities of attainment scrutinized.

The Volitional Medium

Man also approaches God through a third medium, the volitional sphere. By exercising his free moral will, arriving at reasonable ethical decisions and attempting to translate them into facts, man serves God and communes with Him. Halakhic Judaism has placed the main emphasis upon this type of service, which consists in raising natural man to the plateau of the spiritual, harnessing and guiding physiological-psychical man's insensate drives and impulses, and endowing them with meaningful content and purposive directedness. The major part of our *mitzvot ma'asiyyot* (practice of *mitzvot*) is committed to the realization of the great goal of converting the mechanical laws governing our existence into patterns of sacred living, elevating man to a normative-ethical existence, instead of abandoning him to the governance of those mechanical laws. A powerful will is combined with a capacity for the application of theory to reality, for the implementation of norms and their transformation into facts.

Judaism is basically a voluntaristic discipline. It has established the primacy of the will. (Of course, we mean the intelligent, good will, not the blind will of Schopenhauer.) Judaism declared man to be a being who, first of all, wills and then is capable of pursuing the objectives determined by the will, persisting in the expectation that they will be attained. However important the intellect is, the crowning deed of human accomplishment is a very sensitive moral will, which is capable of deciding freely, of choosing the good and of carrying out its decisions. Important is the deed, not the theory, and the deed is the powerful expression of an active moral will, an effort which has not been arrested en route and has not missed its object. Here, Judaism displayed its greatness and ingenuity. One serves God and enters into an intimate relationship with Him by self-actualization on the part of the moral will, by living a moral life, by walking humbly with people, by engaging in deeds of charity, by being just and merciful, generous and kind, by cultivating the truth, by helping others, by disciplining oneself, by taming one's animal desires and impulses, and by introducing axiological worth into the realm of a bodily existence. The Torah did not distinguish in this respect between cult and ethos. One worships God not only by approaching Him directly through cultic ceremonial, by which man addresses himself to God, and which are supposed to serve as a sign-language expressing man's anxiety and longing for the Creator, but also (and perhaps mainly) through moral self-realization and activation. The Decalogue contains nothing cultic. It is throughout an ethical code; its realization constitutes the basic relationship between God and Israel as a nation, as a community of the committed.

The Dialogical Medium

The fourth medium through which communication of man with God is accomplished is dialogue. Both prayer and prophecy are basically dialogues between finitude and infinity. They differ only as to the respective roles assigned to creature and Creator. In prophecy God is the active partner of the dialogue community and man is happy being just a listener, an onlooker, watchful and vigilant; in prayer the roles are reversed. God is the listener and man is the speaker.

Many contemporary conceptions of the prayer service diminish it considerably due to a one-sided preoccupation with its hymnal and thanksgiving elements. Judaism vigorously disagreed with this elimination of petition. On the contrary, Judaism not only retained the so-called selfish prayer in its liturgical texts but considered such prayer the central theme of the service. It suffices to glance through the Bible to become unmistakably aware of the fact that petition is the main form of human prayer. Eliezer, on his journey to Haran, petitioned the Almighty to bestow upon him grace and introduce to him the woman who was chosen for Isaac (Gen. 24:12). Isaac prayed to God and implored Him to grant him offspring (Gen. 25:21). Jacob prayed to God when he was about to meet his brother Esau ("Save me from the hand of my brother, from the hand of Esau" (Gen. 32:9)). The Jews in Egypt prayed and offered their petition to God ("And the children of Israel groaned to God and cried out" (Ex. 2:23)). Moses implored God on numerous occasions (see Ex. 32-33; Num. 14 *inter alia*). Hannah prayed to the Lord that He give her a son (I Sam. 1:10ff). David in his Psalms indulges incessantly in supplication and entreaty. Of course, the Psalms include hymnal (such as Psalm 104) and thanksgiving songs. However, the petition forms the essence of this wonderful book of the Bible. If one should eliminate this aspect, the psalmist would be silenced forever. Even the hymns whose main theme is praise often include passages of solicitation for help and sympathy.

The middle part of the weekday *Amidah*, the silent prayer, is completely devoted to thoughtful petition and consists of thirteen blessings, while the other two parts expressing adoration and gratitude comprise only three blessings each. The blessings of adoration and gratitude serve as a prologue and epilogue, respectively; the central petitions to Him are *avodah she-ba-lev* in action: the service of God and the addressing to Him of our appeal for help. When we investigate other *berakhot* texts, we discover the same selfish overtone of petition to God. Quite frequently the transition from adoring thanksgiving to supplication is so natural that we are not aware of the thematic change that occurs.

For example, *birkot nissu'in* (the marriage benedictions) begin with hymnal adoration: God has created man in His image and ordained his perpetuation. Suddenly, the text goes off on a tangential theme of petition: "Let the barren one rejoice in the gathering of her sons." Sometimes, the *berakhah* itself switches its motif from praise to request. The last *berakhah* of the *birkot nissu'in* is the best illustration. First, we bless God who has created joy, groom and bride; but having started out as a hymn it culminates with a petition: "May the sound of joy soon be heard in the cities of Judah and the streets of Jerusalem..." Other texts display a similar move from initial praise to plea. To take an additional example among many: the central *berakhah* in the *tefillah* of *Yom Tov* or *Shabbat*, which begins either with "*atta behartanu* (You chose us)" or "*atta kiddashta* (You sanctified)", as the case may be. At the outset, we chant our gratitude to the Almighty for choosing us and sanctifying the holy day; we go on to express our sense of exaltedness over the historical role which was assigned to us. We then move on to prayer and supplication, in which we beseech the Almighty to fulfill his covenant and realize the particular message of the holy day.

The reason for the centrality that Judaism has given to the element of petition in the service lies in our philosophy of prayer. *Avodah she-ba-lev*, for all its tendency to express the religious experience as a whole, and particularly its emotional aspect, does also tend to single out a particular state of mind. For when we view the noetic content of prayer we must admit that one emotion is central as far as prayer is concerned— namely the feeling of unqualified dependence. David expressed this experience of complete, absolute, unconditional dependence upon God in his beautiful verses: "If I did not quiet myself like a weaned child upon his mother, verily my soul is like one weaned. Let Israel hope in God now and forever" (Ps. 131:2-3).

Therefore, the understanding of Jewish prayer must give a place of prominence to the idea and to the experience of petition. The following chapter and chapter 10 will focus on the commandment *(mitzvah)* to pray and on the centrality of petition to the fulfillment of that commandment.

❧ Prayer, Petition and Crisis

Actional Mitzvot

To attain a better understanding of the commandment to pray, we must first engage in a halakhic analysis pertinent to *mitzvot* in general. The Halakhah distinguishes between two kinds of *mitzvot*—the actional (*hiyyuv be-ma'aseh*) and the experiential (*hiyyuv she-ba-lev*). The former denotes a norm that is outer-directed and whose fulfillment is achieved through a concrete action in the world of things and physical events. The Halakhah singles out a certain activity within the complex routine engagements, which is in itself insensate and devoid of content, and raises it to the level of religious significance. For instance, holding of the *lulav* on the first day of Sukkot, eating of *matzah* on the first night of Passover, donning of *tefillin* on an ordinary weekday—each is a physical deed consisting only of a muscular activity. Yet, the fact that each is a halakhically mandated act, converts a mechanical performance into a meaningful performance endowed with significance, one that results from its conformity to a transcendental norm. The particular mood of the doer, who may or may not understand its idealizing and purifying power, is not regarded as a component of the religious performance in question. The actional *mitzvot* form a halakhic objective order which is not correlated with a parallel subjective one. The objective action does not point to a corresponding experience, mental attitude, or inner activity. The norm comes into being within the world of events, actions and things, not in the one of feelings, thoughts and volitions. At times God summons not the heart but the hand of man, not his spiritual consciousness but his physical potential.

This doctrine of Halakhah is certainly acceptable to the school of Talmudic scholarship holding the view that *mitzvot einan tzerikhot kavvanah*, that a mitzvah performance is valid even when not accompanied by normative motivation (see *Berakhot* 13a). One who blew the shofar solely for aesthetic reasons—let us say that he enjoyed the sound of the instrument— also is considered to have fulfilled the halakhic norm. According to this view, all the Halakhah is interested in is the mechanical performance, even if it is not indicative or representative of any inner feeling or thought. Yet, even if we accept the opposite view that *mitzvot tzerikhot kavvanah*, that the *mitzvah*-performance must be intentional and motivated by a sense of duty, we would nevertheless maintain that the Halakhah operates with a single order of objective data and does not resort to one sort of parallelism which would coordinate external action with some subjective elements. *Kavvanah*—the intention to which the *mitzvot* are linked—signifies duty-awareness and normative intentionality, as is tersely formulated in the preparatory prayer *hinneni mukhan*, "I hereby ready myself to fulfill the *mitzvah* . . ." (a formula often recited before the specific performance of a *mitzvah*. This duty awareness remains constant and retains its identity even though it accompanies *mitzvot* of a variety of philosophic significance.) The pious Jew pronounces a similar *hinneni mukhan* prior to both eating *matzah* and blowing the *shofar,* notwithstanding that in terms of symbolic interpretation the two *mitzvot* represent opposite attitudes. The *kavvanah* associated with actional *mitzvot* is a peripheral intention and not a central one.

Thus, the actional *mitzvot* operate with materials drawn from the senses and not from our invisible lives of feeling and striving. They do not represent mental qualities, abstract conceptions and inner movements. Action, in these cases, is the beginning and the end of the man-God relationship.

Experiential Mitzvot

In contradistinction to the actional *mitzvot*, which form a single objective series, the experiential *mitzvot* refer to a spiritual act, a state of mind, an inner attitude or outlook. The norm originates not in the world of action but in the world of thought, feeling and volition. The Halakhah enters a new dimension of human life, that of subjectivity and inwardness. In contrast to actional *mitzvot*, the experiential *mitzvot* postulate a way not only of doing but of experiencing as well. The Halakhah attempts to regulate not only the body but also the soul.

Experiential *mitzvot* must be divided into two subgroups. First, there are inward actions that form a single subjective experience without calling for outward action at all. The inner stirring does not press for portrayal or symbolization in objective form and remains shut in, within the human heart, remote from the world of events, wanting in contour and aloof from all concreteness. Sometimes one receives an unlimited amount of pleasure in contemplation that has no practical significance, in a pensive mood devoid of dynamics, in apprehending something that is at an endless distance from actuality and definiteness. The dominant note in such experiences is either their utter sublimity and tenderness, which would be affected if put into the mold of objectification, or their tremendous sweep and power, which does not tolerate fixity and standardization.

Be that as it may, such *mitzvot* are realized by the heart, not by the hand. The activity of the mind is filled with religious worth, but the body does not participate in that realization. We subsume, under this category, the fundamental precepts of our faith, such as the commandment to believe in God's unity, to love and fear Him, to trust in Him, among others. These precepts, using Rabbi Bahya's phrase in his eleventh century work, *Duties of the Heart,* are concerned with the *hovot ha-levavot* (duties of the heart), not with those of the limbs. Faith in God, commitment, and love of Him, do not require specific symbolic actions for the purpose of objectification and manifestation of the inward experience. Maimonides (in the introduction to his *Sefer ha-Mitzvot*) calls such precepts *mitzvot kelaliyot*, general commandments, ones which have no specific correlate in the objective religious sense. The *mitzvot kelaliyot* bear upon the whole body of the law and are related to a mental attitude rather than an outward deed. In short, the general precepts refer to contemplative experiences that do not cross the gulf separating our inner world from that of action.

The second subgroup of experiential commandments, unlike the general precepts discussed above, are specific in nature. They express themselves through a parallel series of activity and experience: of inner movement and outer action. The contemplative experience develops a dynamic uncontrollable force that breaks through the barrier of inwardness into the world of deeds and movement. The Halakhah is no longer satisfied with the inner image, and it demands externalization and actual representation. The purely experiential search ends in action. The religious norm does not work from a single center, but is resident in two parallel orders: subjective and objective responsiveness.

The Halakhah is distrustful of the genuineness and depth of our inner life, because of its vagueness, transience and volatility. Therefore, it has introduced, in the realm of the experiential norms, concrete media through which a religious feeling manifests itself in the form of a concrete act. For instance, the precept of rejoicing on a festival, *simhat Yom Tov*, is realized through a double activity—experiencing the redeeming, uplifting and inspiring joy, on the one hand, and conforming to the external cultic standard of bringing *shelamim* offerings (sacrifices in which the owners partake) and feasting, on the other. The specific physical performances are prescribed, by the Halakhah, as the external symbol of the exalted mood. The same is true of *avelut*, the norm commanding one to mourn for one's deceased relatives. A mourner who has complied scrupulously with the ritual of *avelut* but remained unresponsive to and unaffected by his encounter with death—if the passing of his next of kin did not fill him with gloom—has failed to fulfill the precept of mourning. At the same time, a mourner who neglects the observance of the externals is derelict to his duty, even though he lived through the horror and dismay of coming face to face with nihility.

The outer action required by the Halakhah in this group of experiential precepts is dramatic in nature. One does not just act; he acts something out. The dominant theme of the performance is a great exciting story. The action is kerygmatic, message-bearing. It tells a tale of the human mind and heart, of something wondrous or tragic that occurred in the deep recesses of the I. It is filled with eagerness on the part of the doer to unburden himself of an emotional load, pressing on his frail personality. The action is vehement and fervent, and in its rush and earnestness we see the consuming passion, a soul frightened and exalted, believing and rebelling, making a heroic effort to express the inexpressible.

Thus, halakhic examination reveals the primary characteristic of that group of *mitzvot* which finds expression in parallel action. It is that in each mitzvah we must carefully discriminate between *ma'aseh ha-mitzvah* (the piecemeal process of actual execution) and *kiyyum ha-mitzvah*, compliance with the norm. *Ma'aseh ha-mitzvah* denotes a religious technique, a series of concrete media through which the execution of the *mitzvah* is made possible, while *kiyyum ha-mitzvah* is related to the total effect, to the achievement itself, to the structural wholeness of the norm realization.

There is technique in painting: the proper selection and use of colors, the expert strokes of the brush, and so on. Yet the painting as a piece of art is something different from all these details. It can never be integrated through a piecemeal, additive process, combining the various phases of the execution of the details of the artistic work. It is the personal element, the talent of the artist, the instantaneous creative spark, that makes the work worthwhile from an artistic viewpoint.

A similar perspective illuminates the *kiyyum ha-mitzvah*. It is something personal, intimate, and indefinable. It describes, not mechanical action, but the accomplishment itself, the leap from submission to a norm to freedom which comes with fulfillment. It is a personality-attribute, fixing the position of the doer in the universe of norms and values. *Ma`aseh ha-mitzvah* is a factual, descriptive term; *kiyyum ha-mitzvah* an axiological category.

In the realm of the normative parallelism, the objective construct—the physical act, the ritual components—exhaust themselves in the *ma`aseh ha-mitzvah*. God demanded action from man, and the latter is eager to discharge his commitment. This he can accomplish only through doing what is required of him by way of physical effort. Hence, the observance of the mourning ritual or the bringing of festival offerings constitutes the *ma`aseh ha-mitzvah*. These actions are antecedent to the fulfillment, the *kiyyum*, of the respective norms, which is attained in the depths of a great experience, in a spiritual act, in the hidden movements of an overjoyed, ecstatic heart, or, in the case of mourning, of a downtrodden spirit overcome by shock and dismay.

Thus, the parallelism of act and fulfillment is not to be equated with duplication or replication. The objective and subjective orders represent two aspects, technique and accomplishment, respectively, the preliminary process and fulfillment itself. In the objective sphere the person moves along the periphery of detail and technical media; in the subjective sphere, he performs a movement of recoil, withdrawing from the peripheral and piecemeal action toward the center of instantaneous realization.

The Character and Essence of Prayer

In light of this halakhic analysis, we may now seek to determine the character and essence of *avodah she-ba-lev*. Does *avodah she-ba-lev* exhaust itself in standardized action, in the recital of a fixed text thrice daily, or in an inner experiential reality, in spiritual activity? Is it an actional norm or an experiential one? If it is indeed experiential, under what specific group of experiential norms should it be classified?

The answer to this inquiry was formulated by Maimonides many centuries ago. When introducing the obligation to pray as a Pentateuchal precept that is an aspect of the concept "*U-le-ovdo be-khol levavkhem*," ("to serve Him with all your heart"), he explained the twofold character of *avodah she-ba-lev*:

> Commandment 5 is that He has commanded us that we are to serve Him. This commandment is repeated twice in His words, "And ye shall serve the Lord your God", and "Him shalt thou serve." Now although this commandment also is of the class of general precepts, as we have explained in Root 4, yet there is a specific duty the commandment pertaining to prayer. In the words of the Sifre: "and to serve Him"—this refers to prayer (*Sefer ha-Mitzvot*, Positive Commandment 5).

Maimonides places the precept of *avodah she-ba-lev* within two perspectives: First, there is a purely subjective aspect. The term *avodah she-ba-lev* refers to a spiritual act that is completely divorced from physical involvement. The literal semantics of the term indicate service by the heart. Maimonides calls this kind of commandment general (*kelali*), since no concrete action is required for the norm's realization. Second, Maimonides speaks of the specific subnorm of *avodah she-ba-lev* that is linked with prayer. This aspect of the norm delivers the experience from its amorphous, ephemeral state and achieves its objectification in concrete action. Thus, the fulfillment of the norm is tied to a performance, a parallel action through which experiential actions stir the soul into bodily motion.

In other words, prayer constitutes a basic method of religious representation. It is a mode of representing a sublime mood through sensuous forms, a kind of physical portraiture of invisible experiences. Prayer is the tale of an aching and yearning heart.

We must discriminate between two aspects of *tefillah*: the external one, constituting the formal act of prayer, and the inner experience, which expresses the very essence of the mitzvah. The physical deed of reciting a fixed text serves only as a medium through which the experience finds its objectification and concretion. It is not to be identified with the genuine act of praying, which is to be found in an entirely different dimension, namely, in the great, wondrous God-experience.

Kavvanah (intention), as we have noted, generally requires only normative heedfulness or motivation on the part of the doer—that is to say, the intention to discharge one's duty in accord with God's will, thus not constituting an integral part of the religious gesture. The controversy about *mitzvot tzerikhot kavvanah,* whether *mitzvot* require intention, is confined to the class of objective norms. As far as *tefillah* is concerned, all agree that the physical performance divorced from the inner experience is worthless. Maimonides writes: "Prayer without *kavvanah* is no prayer at all. The man who has prayed without *kavvanah* is duty bound to recite his prayer over again" (*Hilkhot*

Tefillah 4:15). For *kavvanah* with respect to *tefillah* forms the very core of the act; without it prayer would become a meaningless and stereotyped ceremonial. Hence, the *kavvanah* concerning *tefillah* must express itself not in a mere duty-awareness, but in an all embracing and an all-penetrating transcendental experience. One turns toward God with the heart and not merely the lips, with thoughts and not only words. Whatever Maimonides' view is on whether normative intention is required in general, his position on prayer is clear: If *kavvanah* does not represent inward devotion or commitment, it is deprived of significance. No religious performance has occurred.

To review this central point: the very essence of *tefillah* expresses itself in a romance rather than in disciplined action, in a great passionate yearning rather than a limited cold achievement, in a movement of the soul rather than performance of the lips, in an awareness rather than in action, in an inner longing rather than a tangible performance, in silence rather than in loud speech. As we emphasized above, the external elements are indispensable, since the Halakhah always operates with a double series: the subjective and the objective. Certainly one who does not correlate the experience with an objective symbol, in this case the recital of words, is remiss in his duty. However, the external act is clearly but a side, a formal side, of the full state of mind. The latter turns away from the externals and from physical efforts; the individual is captivated by the great vision of the supremely impressive and wondrous. The inner activity, free from reaching out for external accomplishment; the inward look which does not call out for outward deeds; the attention that goes entirely to the unseen and is indifferent to the outer show; in brief—the *avodah she-ba-lev* which ceremonial and decorum seem to hinder—this is the essence of prayer.

Defining the Subjective and Objective in Prayer

Our next task is to analyze the general precept *avodah she-ba-lev* with, on the one hand, its purely subjective elements, and, on the other hand, the specific aspect of *avodah she-ba-lev* that relates to the rituals of prayer. We must pose two questions: First, what does the norm of *avodah she-ba-lev* contain in its universal form; to what kind of state of mind is it related? Second, what does the *kavvanah* associated with the specific experience of prayer mean in philosophical, analytical terms? What are its basic motifs?

As regards our first problem, Maimonides has furnished us with a very detailed description of *avodah she-ba-lev* in its universal form:

> We have already spoken of the various degrees of prophets; we will therefore return to the subject of this chapter, and exhort those who have attained a knowledge of God, to concentrate all their thoughts in God. This is the worship (*avodah*) peculiar to those who have acquired a knowledge of the high truths; and the more they reflect on Him, and think of Him, the more are they engaged in His worship . . . When you have arrived by way of intellectual research at a knowledge of God and His works, then commence to devote yourselves to Him, try to approach Him and strengthen the intellect, which is the link that joins you to Him. Thus Scripture says: "Unto thee it was showed that thou mightest know that the Lord He is God" (Deut. 4:35). Thus, the law distinctly states that the highest kind of worship to which we refer in this chapter, is only possible after the acquisition of the knowledge of God. For it is said: "To love the Lord your God and to serve Him with all your heart and all your soul" (Deut. 11:13), and, as we have shown several

times, man's love of God is identical with his knowledge of Him. The Divine service enjoined in these words must, accordingly, be preceded by the love of God. Our sages have pointed out to us that it is an *avodah she-ba-lev*, which explanation I understand to mean this: man concentrates all his thoughts on the First Intellect (God), and is absorbed in these thoughts as much as possible... It has thus been shown that it must be man's aim, after having acquired the knowledge of God, to deliver himself up to Him, and to have his heart constantly filled with longing after Him. He accomplishes this generally by seclusion and retirement . . .

When we have acquired a true knowledge of God, and rejoice in that knowledge in such a manner, that whilst speaking with others, or attending to our bodily wants, our mind is all that time with God; when we are with our heart constantly near God, even whilst our body is in the society of men; when we are in that state which the Song on the relation between God and man describes in the following words: "I sleep, but my heart waketh; it is the voice of my beloved that knocketh" (Song 5:2)—then we have attained not only the height of ordinary prophets, but of Moses, our Teacher... (*Guide* III:51).

Let us abstract from this idea of intellectualism to which Maimonides subscribed with zeal and ardor. Whether or not the logos, reason, is the exclusive medium of approaching God is not of prime importance for the present discussion. Likewise, we may ignore the ascetic overtones discernible in the Maimonidean description of *avodah she-ba-lev*. They too are a side issue as far as our subject matter is concerned. What we are concerned with is the eidetic (structural) analysis of *avodah she-ba-lev* itself.

The Maimonidean idea of service of the heart is to be seen at two levels: the psychological and the mystical. From the psychological viewpoint, *avodah she-ba-lev* is identical with the state of mind which is called mono-ideism, the giving of attention to one idea exclusively. Our attention to the *mitzvah* is divorced from all other centers of interest and is focused upon a single subject. In other words, *avodah she-ba-lev* borders on total involvement with God and total separation from finite goods and values. It is a type of fixation, however voluntary, that borders on the anomalous, divine madness (*shiggayon*). It is a love that transcends the bounds of reasonableness and sense, and reaches into the paradoxical and the absurd. It is known with certitude that the love of God does not become clearly knit in a man's heart until he is continuously and thoroughly obsessed by it and gives up everything else in the world for it. One serves God with an insane love. (See *Hilkhot Teshuvah* 10:6.)

At a mystical level, *avodah she-ba-lev* is identical with communion, with closeness to God and the ecstatic act of perception of Him. *Devekut* is the transcendence of finitude; it is the extension of the existential experience into the boundlessness of the beyond in the direction of the Supreme Being. The insane, intense stretching forth is fully rewarded by the clarity of vision and apprehension. In a word, *avodah she-ba-lev* describes total involvement with and commitment to God, the exalted awareness of sharing infinity itself.

The element of *tefillah* which expresses this sort of ecstatic mood, a mood of mental entrancement due to the suspension of the trivial and relative and absorption by the great and unconditional, is an aspect of *avodah she-ba-lev* in the universal sense we have discussed. Maimonides defined *kavvanah* for prayer in similar terms, stressing mono-ideism, that is the unification of awareness, and the experience of nearness to the Absolute and Eternal: "Now, what is *kavvanah*? One must free his heart from all other thoughts and regard himself as standing in the presence of God" (*Hilkhot Tefillah* 4:16). Both elements are clearly defined.

Translating this into modern philosophical vocabulary, we would say that *avodah she-ba-lev* covers just one aspect of the total span of an all-embracing religious experience, with its many shafts of light and potential for spiritual energy, seen against the backdrop of a paradoxical existential awareness. In it the leading motifs of the Judaic transcendental relationship of God and man, with all its fluctuations, conflicts and paradox, are closely knotted together. Through *avodah she-ba-lev* the soul longs to recover its resemblance to God, even while it is aware of the dissimilitude that separates the creation from the Creator. Through the medium of *avodah she-ba-lev*, man tries to express his closeness to and endless remoteness from God, his love and his fear, his anguish and his serenity, his unshakable faith and his satanic doubts, his joy and his sorrow, his being and his non-being, his capacity both for achieving greatness and for falling into the abyss of smallness.

Thus, *avodah she-ba-lev* is realized when the awareness of the unseen reality accompanies man through life; when one feels overwhelmed as he stands before the *mysterium tremendum* of Being; when, in each and every movement of one's soul, every stretching of one's muscle, God addresses Himself to man. Then, *avodah she-ba-lev* tears down the barriers separating the mundane from the Divine, the profane from the sacred, the mechanical from the inspiring; it converts life from a given, a factum, to an exalted and uplifting heroic actus, from a grant to a challenge.

Maimonides emphasized that the commandment *U-le-ovdo be-khol levavkhem* (Deut. 11:13), to serve Him with all your heart, belongs to the class of general precepts (those which apply not to a specific case and act but contain a norm whose innate applications are all-inclusive and refer to the total attitude of man toward God) and that *tefillah* represents only one facet of this basic precept of *avodah she-ba-lev*. The quotation from the midrashic sources, which Maimonides utilizes in order to prove his thesis regarding the Pentateuchal character of prayer, supports our viewpoint that *avodah she-ba-lev* exceeds the narrow confine of formal prayer and liturgic performance. Studying the Torah is also included, since through the acts of learning and teaching man expresses his inner religious self. Whenever the true God-seeking self appears on the threshold of our objective world, the miracle of *avodah she-ba-lev* is achieved.

Is Prayer for Everyone?

However, our inquiry into the essence of *kavvanah* has not yet come to an end. A serious problem comes to the fore. It can be formulated as follows. Prayer, indeed, is the symbolic portrayal of a range of experiences that form the ecstatic state of mind. Is such an exalted experience something in which every human being may share; or is it confined to the religious genius—a curious and unique type of personality who is capable of attaining this ecstatic state of mind, of rapture and unification, a personality who rejects what seems clearly, logically and tangibly to be the natural order, for the sake of tending a reality which is beyond one's grasp? Is prayer only for the mystic? We, in contrast to the mystic, are all physically and mentally children of this external concrete world and therefore, if this be true, cannot make the leap from the sensuous and real into the transcendent and absolute. Hence, *avodah she-ba-lev*, in the Maimonidean description, is an esoteric adventure, one that is not understandable to the average person. Saints or mystics, whom God has blessed with an oversensitized nature, with the capacity for violent and indelible emotions, with an exalted sense of perceptions and fantasy—they may follow the mystical way, devoting their existence to the Infinite. But we may not be able to do so.

What, then, does *avodah she-ba-lev* mean for us, with our unmystical bent of mind that tends toward the real and practical? Can we achieve the *kavvanah* of *tefillah* in our ordinary modest way though we are not able to embark upon the great and strange adventure of the spirit? Of course the answer must be formulated in the affirmative, for otherwise *tefillah* would be the exclusive privilege of the imaginative genius, the mystic, and, as such, would be denied to ordinary man. Such an assertion would contradict the very essence of the Halakhah, which is an exoteric discipline to be practiced by the philosopher and simpleton, the poet and the dull person alike.

Unless *tefillah* as a Halakhic norm can find a place within the frame of reference of the normal mentality, and lend itself to realization by every human being, regardless of his spiritual limitations, its meaning to us could never be more than academic and remote since it would contain a *contradictio in adjecto*—a Halakhic norm entrusted to an esoteric group, to the select few. Moses bidding farewell to his people said: "You stand today before God, all of you, your leaders... and all the people of Israel" (Deut. 29:9). The Torah is the common property of the Jews: all classes, the elite, the elders and the leaders, as well as the plebeian. The woodchopper and the water drawer must be assured that they, too, may realize its norms.

However embarrassing the problem is, it should not be considered insoluble. I dare say there is a solution that might save *tefillah* from becoming a Halakhic absurdity. The clue to this solution we may find through a careful analysis of the *Amidah* (the silent prayer, the *Shemoneh Esreh*).

The Structure of Prayer

As we noted, the *Amidah* rests upon three liturgical motifs: the hymn, the petition and the thanksgiving: *shevah, bakkashah* and *hoda'ah*. The first three blessings represent hymnal praise; the middle thirteen, the petitional aspect; the last three, thanksgiving service. Although the standardized liturgical text of *Amidah* is a Rabbinic creation, Maimonides maintains that its triple motif is a Pentateuchal institution

(*Hilkhot Tefillah* 1:2). For Moses, in his famous entreaty to enter the land of Israel (Deut. 3:23-25), begins with praise of the Lord, and his prayer has served as a guiding motif in the formulation of the *Amidah*. In the book of Psalms we find a similar textual arrangement. *Hallel* (Ps. 113-118, recited on Festivals and the New Moon), for instance, also begins with hymnal adoration, turns to supplication, and concludes with thanksgiving.

Apparently, the triple pattern reflects the inner experience, the subjective correlate of prayer. In the light of this premise, I would suggest that the main concern of the Halakhah is this threefold motif within the total God-experience which is explicated in the physical act of praying. Obviously, other beams of light within the experiential spectrum possess a high potentiality for the mystic and religious genius, but they are remotely related to the ordinary person. These three motifs—these three rays—offer remedial and inspiring energy for everybody. Therefore, they were singled out and spelled out in our silent prayer.

The petitional, hymnal and thanksgiving aspects of prayer portray three experiential conceptions and spiritual movements: the conception of *mi-ma'amakkim* (*de profundis*), the crisis cry from the depths; the concept of *kevod Malkhuto (majestas Dei)* the majesty of God; and the concept of *hesed Elokim* (*caritas Dei*), the grace of God. Petition flows from an aching heart which finds itself in existential depths; hymn emerges from an enraptured soul gazing at the *mysterium magnum* of creation; thanksgiving is sung by the person who has attained, by the grace of God, redemption.

Petition and Distress

Mystics, philosophers, aesthetes and naturalists alike consider petitionary prayer an unworthy part of the service, a remnant of magical religion, when the savage bartered with his

gods and tried to reach a *quid pro quo* deal with them. As they
see it, the development of religious thought and the purging of
all magical cultic elements, on the one hand, and the emergence
of natural sciences founded upon the unalterability of the causal
nexus, on the other hand, undermined selfish prayer. As a
result, petitionary prayer lost its meaning and rationale in the
opinion of many. We have already observed how radically
Judaism diverged from this viewpoint.

Tefillah, according to Halakhah, is closely knit with the
experience of *tzarah*, distress or—to be more loyal to the literal
semantics—constriction; it means finding oneself in distressingly narrow straits. Many passages in the Bible confirm this
premise. King Solomon defined prayer as the outcry of a person
in the dark night of disaster: "Should Your people Israel be rout-
ed by an enemy because they have sinned against You, and then
turn back to You and acknowledge Your name, and they offer
prayer and supplication to You in this House" (I Kings 8:33).
Only distress warrants prayer. If the mind is not haunted by
anxiety, not plagued by *tzarah*, narrowness and constriction, if
neither fear nor forlornness assault the mind, then prayer is a
futile gesture. Nahmanides (Ramban) in his annotations to the
Sefer ha-Mitzvot (Positive Commandment 5), disagreed with
Maimonides' (Rambam's) view that there is a Biblical norm
mandating the recital of daily prayer. He concurred with him,
however, that in *et tzarah*, in troublesome and critical times,
there is a Biblical commandment of prayer. Thus, he admits
that the Torah posits the significance and meaningfulness of
tefillah as worship of God.

Maimonides, too, was aware of the interrelatedness of
tefillah and *tzarah*. At the beginning of *Hilkhot Ta'anit,* he singled out the moment of *tzarah*: "It is a commandment to cry out
and blow the trumpets ... whenever trouble befalls the community" (1:1). Even in *Hilkhot Tefillah*, Maimonides implicitly
hinted at the *mi-ma'amakkim* or *tzarah* motif when he wrote
that petition must express "plea and entreaty, *be-bakkashah u-*

bi-tehinah," that one must spell out his need in prayer (1:3). If, however, one does not lack anything; if all his desires are gratified and he feels contented and happy, prayer becomes an absurd performance.

Surface and Depth Crisis

The controversy between Nahmanides and Maimonides does not revolve about the conjunction of prayer and *tzarah*. They are in agreement that *tzarah* underlies prayer. They differ, however, about the substance of the experience of *tzarah* itself. The word *mi-ma'amakkim* is in the plural, and one may speak of two distinct and incommensurate *tzarah* conceptions, of two ways of falling into the depths: first, the experience of the surface *tzarah*, the external, objective, impersonal fall; and second, the experience of depth *tzarah*, the existential, personal fall.

Many a time a crisis develops independently of man, brought about in the main by environmental forces which are insensate, mechanical, and quite often not sympathetic to man and his aspirations. This crisis, this *tzarah*, strikes man suddenly, uninvited by the people who succumb to its crushing force. Their plight is obvious, exposed to the public eye, its apprehension as natural as the perception of lightning or thunder. Man does not have to meditate, contemplate, or employ detective skill in order to realize that his very existence is menaced, that the outlook for the future is dismal, and that the chances of extricating himself from such a predicament are slim. This is basically a surface feeling which borders almost on the instinctive, mechanical, passive perception of pain. Under the category of surface *tzarah* we may classify all forms of conventional suffering: illness, famine, war, poverty, loss of physical freedom, and, last but not least, death. All these evils strike man with the force of a hurricane and sweep him off his very existential foundation.

The external fall of man usually occurs at a communal level. *Tzarah* is an impersonal experience which strikes man from outside his existence, it affects not one but many. A famine, epidemic, or war hits groups of people. Many share the experience of distress; many die simultaneously; many take sick at the same time; many starve and stand in bread lines. Communities of the suffering and distressed are formed. They can be found in the hospitals, in the funeral parlors, in the jails, in the slums, on the waterfront and on the Bowery. Therefore, when man is involved in surface crises, the Torah recommends communal prayer. The feeling of sympathy forges a sense of fellowship in prayer and *tzarah*. That is why Maimonides speaks in terms of *tzibbur* (community) (*Hilkhot Ta'anit* 1:1 and *Hilkhot Tefillah* 8:1), and the Halakhah operates with concepts such as *tefillat ha-tzibbur* (prayer of the community). The *tzarah* assumes a public character and the response to the Divine experience is a collective one.

In contradistinction to these surface crises, the depth crisis addresses metaphysical, unknown, undefined and clandestine personal distress. The crisis is encountered in the strangeness of human destiny, of which man is not aware at all unless he is willing to acquaint himself with it. Such a crisis is not brought about by extraneous factors, or precipitated by coincidental entanglements of man in distressingly complex situations. Nor is the experience imposed upon him willy nilly with the elemental force of the natural storm. This type of crisis is searched out and discovered by man and accepted by him freely. It is not something which man tries to protect himself from, into which man is dragged compulsorily because he is stupid and ignorant, as may be the case with illness, famine or war. (If mankind progressed more we would perhaps be able to control these plagues.) Rather it is an experience of complete bankruptcy and failure, which stems from the deepest insight of man—as a great spiritual personality, endowed with Divine wisdom and vision—into his own reality, fate and destiny. Man is not thrown into this kind of crisis but finds it within himself. It is not of natural, social, economic or environmental, but instead of existential-metaphysical origin.

Human existence exhausts itself in the experience of crisis, in the continual discovering of oneself in distress, in the steady awareness of coming closer and closer to the brink of utter despair, the paradoxical concept of being born out of nothingness and running down to nothingness. This is a part of the ontic consciousness of man. The factum expressed in the two words "I am" is an incomplete sentence. We must always qualify it by adding two words: "I am in distress." Judaism wants man to discover the tragic element of his existence, to place himself voluntarily in distressing narrowness, to explicate and bring to the fore the deep-seated crisis in his very existence. Surely man must fight courageously against the extraneous surface crisis. Judaism has charged man with the task of improving creation, of confronting evil and destructive forces, of protecting himself against disease and natural catastrophes, approaching the world with an optimistic philosophy of activism.

The distinction between the attitude of modern existentialism and the Judaic view of the depth crisis is that Judaism advocates distress without anguish. Indeed, one must combat evil and the forces that produce the external crisis. Judaism, handing down to man an optimistic philosophy of activism, charged him with the task of improving the work of God, of eliminating all destructive forces and protecting oneself against disease and other natural catastrophes. With respect to the inner crisis, however, which is rooted in depth-experience, man was told not only that he should not try to disengage himself from his involvement in it but, on the contrary, that he should deepen and accept it. For the very essence of his ontic awareness is thus an exercise in crisis, a process of growth in the experience of crisis.

Out of the depths in which the individual finds himself, one calls upon God in seclusion and loneliness. The existential, passional experience is not shared by the thou, however close he is to the I, since it is an integral part of the existential awareness, which is singular, and hence inexpressible in the universal terms through which we communicate our standardized experiences. No one but the sufferer himself is involved in this deeply human anguish and conflict. It is the sufferer whose awareness oscillates between bliss and pain, in the great negation of the finite that rises out of its confrontation by the infinite. Neither spouse nor child nor parent may understand and sympathize with the lonely individual when his existential experience is at a low ebb, when trials, doubts and inhibitions abound. The prayer echoing the depth crisis of a questing soul emerges from seclusion, from out of the loneliness of the individual whom everybody save God has abandoned: "For my father and mother have abandoned me and God will take me in" (Ps. 27:10). The psalmist speaks of such suffering—the situation of the afflicted person, overwhelmed by his pain, who pours out his complaint before the Lord.

Universal Depth-Crisis Awareness

Each person can excavate the root of his depth crisis, his extraordinary loneliness, if only he tries to understand one unalterably cruel reality. It is that man never emerges victorious from his combat; total triumph is not his destiny. Even when he seems to win the engagement, he is defeated in the very moment that triumph is within his reach. This paradox of our existence manifests itself in this strange experience: at the very instant we complete the conquest of a point of vantage we are tossed back onto the base from where we began our drive. The Divine curse pronounced at the dawn of human existence hovers over all human endeavor. Whatever man may plant, he must reap thorns: "Thorns and thistles shall it bring forth to thee and thou shalt eat the herb of the field" (Gen. 3:18).

Man is engaged in combat on many fronts: physical, economic, social, intellectual, religious. Quite often he lives with the illusion that he has succeeded in winning the battle, that he has raised himself above the insensateness of his environment, that he will harvest a rich crop, that he has unburdened himself of the curse of failure and defeat. This illusion perhaps represents the philosophy of materialism, of aggressive man having faith in himself, moving from victory to victory. Nonetheless, every accomplishment, however great and praiseworthy, contains the prickly seed of its negation.

The reason for man's failure lies in the discrepancy between his creative fantasy and the objective means of self-fulfillment that are at his disposal. While his boundless fantasy expresses itself in accents of endless desire and vast activity, the tools with which he tries to accomplish his goals are limited, since they belong to the finite order of things and forces. Man desires infinity itself yet must be satisfied with a restricted, bounded existence. When he reaches out, he anticipates the endless and boundless, enrapturing himself with the vision of unlimited opportunities. At the hour of achievement, however, he finds himself hemmed in by finitude. The anticipation and the realization lie in different dimensions. Man always loses the final battle.

Jacob, on his way to meet Esau (Gen. 32), wrestled with the mysterious antagonist throughout the dark night, lonely and abandoned by everybody. Did he win the battle? Yes and no. The adversary could not prevail against him; he could not destroy Jacob. But Jacob, at the hour of triumph, when he held his antagonist convulsively fast, felt also defeated; his thigh was out of joint and he therefore limped. Jacob understood that only the Divine blessing could assure him success and victory, could disperse the gloom of the haunted night of conflict and anguish. Jacob prayed for this, unwilling to let the adversary go without his blessing.

This strange scene of Jacob wrestling with the angel is restaged in everyone's life. For man is always in need, and prayer is welcomed by God and man wherever there is need. *Avodah she-ba-lev*, the worship of the heart reflected in prayer, finds its full exoteric expression in the spiritual act of lifting up one's eyes—the inner cry of dependence upon God, the experience of complete absolute dependence portrayed by the psalmist: "I lift my eyes towards the mountains; from where will come my aid?" (Ps. 121:1).

When man is in need and prays, God listens. One of God's attributes is *shomea tefillah*: "He who listens to prayer." Let us note that Judaism has never promised that God accepts all prayer. The efficacy of prayer is not the central term of inquiry in our philosophy of *avodah she-ba-lev*. Acceptance of prayer is a hope, a vision, a wish, a petition, but not a principle or a premise. The foundation of prayer is not the conviction of its effectiveness but the belief that through it we approach God intimately and the miraculous community embracing finite man and his Creator is born. The basic function of prayer is not its practical consequences but the metaphysical formation of a fellowship consisting of God and man.

Man is always in need because he is always in crisis and distress. Inner distress expresses itself in man's disapproval of himself. This awareness is of a metaphysical origin, although it may be manifested at an individual-psychological, social-institutional or political level. Man is dissatisfied with himself and he lacks faith in the justifiability and legitimacy of his existence. Somehow, every human being, great or small, however successful and outstanding, loses every day afresh his ontic fulcrum (the equilibrium of his being), which he tries steadily to recover. He feels the paradox involved in an existence which has been imposed upon him in an unexplained way, and which finally betrays and deserts him in the same absurd manner: "Against your will were you born, against your will do you live, and against your will do you die" (*Avot* 4:29). Even the simplest mind may perceive and comprehend this existential tragic aspect of man.

❧ The Human Condition and Prayer

As we have seen, prayer is related to *tzarah*, to the feeling of distress and adversity. Petition presupposes need. In what concrete terms can we present the depth-experience of the metaphysical crisis in man to the average reader, who lacks philosophical training and whose thinking and feelings are not related to a metaphysical frame of reference?

The awareness of distress manifests itself in a variety of experiences. These experiences are characteristic of everyday life; they are not the province of the spiritual virtuoso alone. They are illustrative of the manner in which all human beings are brought to the awareness of depth-crisis.

The following analysis will touch upon some elements of the human condition. These include distressing experiences such as boredom, sin and shame, on the one hand, and orientations to the world, such as the aesthetic, the cognitive and the ethical, on the other. Reflection on these experiences, among others, brings man to an awareness of a need beyond that of the surface-crisis. The aesthetic orientation, when it overcomes the ethical, is at the root of sin, with all of its distressful features.

Yet, as we shall see, the aesthetic has an important role to play both in human life and in the prayer experience as well, in the hymn of praise and thanksgiving.

The Curse of Boredom

Let us begin our discussion of crisis and the human condition with an analysis of the feeling of boredom, which has become the great disease of our modern society. Man is bored. Hundreds of millions of dollars are spent on his entertainment and amusement. He pays enormous sums to anyone who can elicit a smile from him and make him forget his daily worries. What are these worries? Poverty, sickness, persecution, physical pain? None of these. His main worry is existence itself. He is dissatisfied with what he is doing, with his job, trade or profession. He hates the routine of getting up at 7, catching the 7:45 train, and arriving at the office, where one meets the same people and discusses the same affairs. He finds no joy in what he is doing; he wants to free himself from his daily obligations and activities. He resents the repetition, which is basically a natural phenomenon. He is the most miserable of creatures because he is confined to a cyclic existence which keeps on retracing its steps afresh; for he knows what he is going to do next and what is expected of him. He travels to far-off places, because he is tired of his hometown, with its familiar surroundings, and he engages in an incessant quest for new experiences and stimuli. Of course, all his attempts to break up the monotony and introduce change into repetitious existence are futile. For there is nothing in creation that can offer man something new, exciting and fascinating. He soon realizes that whatever he was looking for does not exist and he comes home, back to his old surroundings and duties. He chases a mirage that recedes endlessly upon his approach.

Basically, this boredom is the consequence of the primal curse with which paradisiacal man was burdened when he rebelled against his Master: "In the sweat of your brow you will eat bread" (Gen. 3:19). These words convey the idea of a life that is not only hated but joyless, the idea of work from which there is no escape, the curse of uniformity and boredom. Man is engaged in a steady rebellion against monotony and strives for change and renewal. The great controversy between the Pre-Socratic thinkers Parmenides and Heraclitus, about the essence of being, left its imprint upon all of Greek philosophy, down to the Stoics and the Epicurean school. Heraclitus held that being expresses itself in continuous movement, metamorphosis, change and flux, while Parmenides championed identity and persistence. This controversy was decided by human beings, emotionally and ontologically, in favor of Heraclitus. Man rejects abstract patterns.

This curse of disapproval affecting man's mode of existence manifests itself in a twofold way. Man hates the work in which he is engaged and seeks to free himself from the so-called bondage: one looks for an escape-route which would somehow bring him to the haven of an unfettered existence. This is exactly the illusion that entertainment tries to create for man, at least for a few short moments. Alternatively, man commits himself unconditionally to work in the hope that more accomplishments, greater successes, more fantastic conquests will fill one's being with joy and contentment. One says to himself: I hate my work now, because the attainments are meager and I have not realized my life's ambition, which is indefinable. However, when I shall succeed in fulfilling my destiny, I shall find happiness.

Man, because of a desire for freedom, becomes more and more enslaved. He would like to liberate himself from all the restrictions of a Parmenidean existence. He desires a limitless multitude of experiences and is indiscriminate about how he attains them. He seeks changes of circumstance, panorama, friends, and objects of enjoyment. What delighted him the day before is obsolete today, and what he indulges in now will lose its attraction with the rise of the morning star. New vistas, strange horizons, unique experiences, unknown ends, lure him from the security and warmth of his homestead. He becomes drunk with the endless opportunities which imagination paints before his mind's eye and he does not want to survey the landscape twice from the same spot. What he wants is a different sunrise every morning.

The awareness of a stable, persistent Parmenidean existence is supplanted by a daemonic, manic craving for vanities and unreal boundlessness. In this imagination, fixed persistent forms and designs disappear into a hyletic mass of experience. Everything is enjoyed for a moment and thrown away the next, nothing is at a standstill, and everything is engaged in movement, rushing on like a powerful stream toward the unknown and unexplored. Fantasy surrounds the experience of man with the halo of change, and man rides upon the crest of a tide that rolls on and on until it breaks down at the immovable shore.

The Cognitive and Ethical Gestures

The conflict between the Parmenidean and the Heraclitean awareness can be equated with the discrepancy between the cognitive-ethical gesture and the aesthetic experience. The cognitive and the ethical are Parmenidean types. The man engaged in the search for truth is always aware of the fixity of the natural law and of his intellectual capacity to conceive it. He employs methods that are basically unalterable and seeks to arrive at an eternal truth. His thoughts move along definite and clear-cut lines. There is no daemonic element of adventure, and there is no illusion of boundlessness and of a wealth of experience that he may embrace and for which he can reach out with both hands. The scientist makes his way, slowly and painstakingly; what is needed is perseverance and extraordinary patience. Let us not forget that the scholar builds the new upon the old. He cannot afford to forget what he experienced in the past. Whatever he discovers is related to a definitive, relational frame of reference, and incorporated as part of a categorical system that very seldom undergoes radical changes. One cannot restart scientific inquiry every morning from the beginning, and one can ill-afford to tear up the blueprint prepared by those who have inquired into reality before us. And what kind of reality does the scientist construe? A relational, formal, monotonous cosmic drama, whose single acts or scenes are abstract entities, whose essence is to be found not in themselves but in behavior towards other entities. The scientifically constructed world, purged of color and sound and qualitative content, empty, uniform, dark and cold in its majestic mathematical terms, is hardly a place for the hero of adventure and change. Science has accepted a philosophy of identity for nature.

The moral person believes in some deontic principles, in strict duties, which are not subject to change and transformation. The ethical law, unaltered, persists in her majestic dignity forever. It is binding at all times, without taking into account the peculiar mind of the individual or the temper of the community. The infinite moral will is not affected by the whimsical turn of events. It pursues just one goal—its realization. The ethical person decides in favor of the norm many times a day and does not become bored or tired of repeating the same act hundreds of times, whenever his conscience commands him to do so. When I come across a burning house where a helpless child has been trapped, I must hasten to rescue the victim, and it would be a criminal folly on my part to desist on the grounds that I have already saved five other children the same day, and I am bored with the continued climbing and carrying of the children overcome by fire.

The crux of the ethical norm exhausts itself in the awareness of continuity and identity, of a life which is a steady engagement in one kind of performance—that of doing good. There is no need for change or recreation. The ethical consciousness does not have to offer continually new stimuli, new vision and varied experience. It realizes itself in one great experience—the fulfillment of one universal law: thou shalt not. In fixing an existential axis around which the human personality revolves, the basic ethical idea excludes transience and introduces permanence, eliminates kaleidoscopically changing patterns and insists upon persistence and stability. The ethos expresses itself in order, in constancy, and in lawful process.

To summarize: the intellectual person and the ethicist accept a Parmenidean ontology.

The Aesthetic Type

In contrast to these representatives of the logos and the ethos, the aesthetic type personifies the Heraclitean mode of existence. By the aesthetic, I understand the all-inclusive human experience by virtue of which one apprehends oneself and the surrounding world as an immediate, constant contact with reality at the qualitative, sensible level. In the aesthetic he expresses his craving for the hedonic, and in it he finds the fulfillment of his sensuality. The aesthetic gesture is a sensuous experience, as the mere etymological connotation of the Greek word *aesthesis* conveys. Beauty is apprehended, not comprehended; the harmonious form is perceived, not conceived. In the aesthetic world, unlike the intellectual world, there are no abstractions. Everything is tangible and approachable to man in aesthetic terms.

The aesthetic engagement, in contradistinction to the intellectual and moral, is a non-teleologic activity. The intellect or the will intends to realize a goal which is determined by the particular philosophy of the individual performing the intellectual or moral act. That goal could be, for example, usefulness, perfection, truth as an ideal, the absolute idea, and the like. The aesthete, on the other hand, does not search for a goal which is transcendent to the aesthetic occupation itself. Man no longer views some beautiful object because he expects it to be useful to him, or for the sake of any other end. He writes lyrics and profound novels, composes music, paints landscapes, builds magnificent structures, acts in thrilling plays, not in order to gain something which is outside of his reach, but for the sheer pleasure of so doing. The final objective and goal of the aesthete is his own self; the aesthetic consciousness delights in the gaze and in the love of itself.

There is something of the narcissist in every aesthete, not excluding the genius. He is selfish, egocentric, many a time vain and capricious. Form exhausts every creative fiber in his personality; the content is of little significance. The word is everything—the meaning is not relevant. The harmony of perception fascinates the aesthete, the synthesis of thought or action does not intrigue him. He works to feel the world; he does not intend to understand or to redeem it.

The aesthete represents only himself; the entire creation centers around him. His self is raised almost to cosmic proportions. Hence, there is no need for an extraneous ideal, for being anchored to some fixed standard. Since the self has become universal, everything reverts to this great mind, which excels above other men. Yet the self-gazing of the aesthete is not to be confused with the self-reckoning of the moralist. The latter approaches himself critically; he tries to assess himself, to weigh his deeds, to account for his conduct, to discover himself. While preoccupied with this process of cognition, he tries to attain the impossible by separating himself, as the judge, observer and knower, from the one who is being judged, watched and recognized.

Actually, in speaking of self-knowledge, the reflexive pronoun "himself" does not convey the real significance of the action. One does not recognize or gaze intellectually at himself, since every cognitive act presupposes the dual arrangement of person and object, of a knower and something to be known. To experience self-knowledge implies a contradiction that cannot be done away with. Every attempt to gain a cognitive insight into oneself is tantamount to an act of self-objectification and estrangement. The person who is under scrutiny, epistemologically speaking, is no longer a part of the self-whole. He finds himself encountering a self that watches and examines him, and this self is a disinterested and detached intellect who, only a while ago, was himself, but who in a strange way dissolved the bond of identity. One cannot stand in the presence of himself unless a mysterious estrangement occurs and personal unity comes to an end. In short, in every act of self-cognition there is epistemological division of the self into person-subject (the knower) and person-object (the known). When the person is present to himself as an unknown something, waiting for the inquiring intellect to grasp him, he is aware that he is no longer a part of himself—alas, he is no longer a self at all; selfhood turns into thinghood, subject into object.

The aesthete, however, when he indulges in self-reflection and self-gazing, does not make the effort of objectification and self-projection into an outside world of thinghood, but rather retreats more and more into himself. He refuses to estrange himself from the very self with whom he was united. Therefore, when the aesthete, the artist, speaks of himself he does so in terms of pure subjectivity. He does not try to recognize himself in an objective manner, but intoxicates himself with self-admiration and adoration, gazing into himself with the candor and detachment of the scholar examining a strange object, since his self has been, in the expression coined by one theologian, expanded to "a world self."* Nothing else exists; there is one world, which reflects himself. The aesthete cannot live in a world of monotony and sterility. He craves unregulated changing designs of living, artistic patterns that are freed from the conventional and the standardized; he yearns for a life delivered from the bondage of the routine. He is self-centered and retreats

---

* "World self" corresponds to the German *Weltseele*, a common term in the philosophy and religious thought of Kant's immediate successors usually translated as "world soul." *–ed.*

into his own subjectivity. He rejects all objective, fixed, self-repeating experiences and searches for the mutable, the new and the unknown. Let us not forget that while the intellect and the will are bent on the order and ontological or ethical references, the sensuous drive is stimulated by hyletic experience (the experience of the unformed), by moving from the old to the new, from the stable to the changeable, from the sedate and simple to the shocking and complicated, from the daily routine to the surprising and unexpected.

Boredom is thus an aesthetic phenomenon. The aesthetic man is resentful of identity and uniformity. He craves a life iridescent with hedonic vanity, replete with ever-changing, colorful beauty. He is tired of the repetitious and monotonous, of the duty which is always the same, of the thought which is abstract and devoid of the colorful, of a life committed to one goal, moving along a straight path, without inviting adventure and without pursuing the hedonic and the daemonic. The aesthete does not understand the rule that a charitable deed, if called for, must be repeated a hundred times.

The ethicist would find boredom an alien experience. For the aesthete, by contrast, the reason to engage in the doing of good is that this preoccupation pleases his sense of beauty; he acts under the guidance of the aesthetic consciousness, not under pressure of his conscience. Hence he is liable to be overcome fairly quickly by boredom and mental fatigue. Constant repetition of a deed dulls his sensitivity and alertness. This conflict between the cognitive, ethical and aesthetic types expresses itself in a basic schism within the cultured mind of the human personality. The theoretician and ethicist in him are at war with the aesthete.

Domination by the Aesthetic—Sin

Sin, according to our world formula, is engendered when the aesthete emerges victorious from the conflict described above, and primacy is accorded to the experience of beauty. Whenever acts of charity and cognitive occupation become an aesthetic performance, stripped of the teleological aspiration—self centered, self indulgent and self pleasing, then sin is born.

Indeed Maimonides (*Guide* 1:2) and Nahmanides (Commentary to Gen. 2:9) interpret the original sin in terms of an aesthetic life supplanting a cognitive-ethical one. Let us review what Maimonides has to say about paradisiacal man. Maimonides stresses, at the very outset, that man, insofar as his intellectual and moral capacities are concerned, was perfect before he committed the original sin.

> The intellect, which was granted to man as the highest endowment, was bestowed on him before his disobedience. With reference to this gift, the Bible states that "man was created in the form and likeness of God." On account of this gift of intellect, man was addressed by God, and received His commandments, as it is said "And the Lord God commanded Adam" for no commandments were given to the brute creation or to those who are devoid of understanding (*Guide* 1:2).

Man is both an intellectual and ethical being. In distinguishing between the two contrasting pairs of *emet ve-sheker* (truth and falsehood) and *tov va-ra* (good and evil), Maimonides does not discriminate between theoretical truth and falsity and moral right and wrong, as many historians have erroneously assumed. (See the English translation of the *Guide* by H. Friedlander, who accepted this interpretation.) Instead, he set up an opposition between the cognitive-ethical truth and falsity, on the one hand, and propriety and impropriety, what is pleasing or displeasing in an aesthetic sense, on the other hand. The terms *tov va-ra* constitute homonyms in Hebrew, having both ethical and aesthetic connotations. On the one hand *tov* means the ethically good and right ("To do the *tov* and righteous in the eyes of God" (Deut. 6:18); "You are *tov* and cause *tov;* instruct me in Your laws" (Ps. 119:68)). On the other hand it signifies also the handsome, good looking, pleasing and nice (Gen. 24:16, 41:5; Ex. 2:2; Esther 2:7).

Maimonides translates the words *tov va-ra*, in the story of the original fall, as meaning the pleasant and unpleasant, the comfortable and uncomfortable, or the delightful and ugly. He says so explicitly when he continues, in explaining the fall:

> After man's disobedience, however, when he began to give way to desires that had their source in his imagination and to the gratification of his bodily appetites as it is said "And the wife saw that the tree was good for food and delightful to the eyes... " (Gen. 3:6) (*Guide* 1:2).

Apparently, Maimonides interprets the first adjectival determinative in the continuation of the verse, *le-haskil,* in the sense of success rather than knowledge, meaning that the tree is good for success (cf. Josh. 1:7-8; I Sam. 18:5f).

What caused man's fall is his giving preference to the sensuous, delightful and pleasing over the true, at both intellectual and ethical levels. The passage about Adam and Eve opening their eyes and knowing they were naked, which Maimonides quotes in order to substantiate his interpretation of the fall, confirms our theory that Maimonides is dealing with the aesthetic experience. Maimonides writes:

> When Adam was yet in a state of innocence and was guided solely by reflection and reason, on account of which it is said: "Thou hast made him little lower than the angels," he was not at all able to follow or understand the principles of *mefursamot* (aesthetic propriety and impropriety) (*Guide* 1:2).

I wish to stress that we must not equate the Maimonidean exposition of the original sin with the scholastic theory of concupiscence. While the latter stresses the actual overindulgence and voluptuousness, singling out lust as the main source of evil, Maimonides places the emphasis upon a tendency, a philosophy of life on the part of man and his longing for and overestimating the importance of the pleasing and beautiful. For Maimonides, the sin manifests itself in a false axiological assessment of man's experiences, thus giving priority to the aesthetic behavior, not so much in an orgiastic mode of life.

Sin and Shame

The most manifest impropriety is to appear in a state of nudity. According to Adam's ideas before the fall, nudity was not unbecoming; he could not comprehend why it should be unbecoming. That is because the shame of nudity is of an aesthetic origin, not of an ethical nature. The nude body is both pleasing and disturbing, beautiful (the culture of the body) and ugly. The feeling that is caused by the exposure of intimate parts of the body has nothing in common with the feeling of shame pursuant to the commission of an immoral act, which involves elements of self-accusation, remorse and contrition. The shame of nudity expresses an emotion of aesthetic abhorrence and aversion. It is a feeling of embarrassment rather than shame in the moral sense of the term. The difference between these two emotions is very conspicuous. Embarrassment is basically a relational experience—I am embarrassed in the presence of others. When a man is alone, he does not feel embarrassed, for that emotion expresses the community-mindedness of man.

Ethical shame, by contrast, is independent of man's relational circumstances. Even a Robinson Crusoe on a solitary island would feel ashamed if he happened to perpetrate something immoral. Shame does not convey, as embarrassment does, fear of encountering contempt on the part of others, but manifests the awareness of one's own worthlessness and ontic despair. It is a metaphysical experience, whereas embarrassment is a social one.

Until the fall, man was a cognitive-ethical being: his aesthetic cravings were apparently subordinated to these basic drives in him. Upon eating from the Tree of Knowledge, man chose the aesthetic way of life and departed from that of abstract thought and unqualified imperative. The magnitude of the loss was tremendous, since he forfeited the ability of thinking in purely abstract terms, and became, even in his cognitive processes, a slave to sensibility. The word *tov va-ra* (good and evil) conveys not the idea of knowledge but that of feeling, of indulging, of enjoying or suffering or establishing contact. (*Da'at* in this sense appears in Gen. 4:1 and Ex. 2:25.)

Aesthetic Experience and Purpose

Boredom is the wages of sin, of an existence overcome by aesthetic enthusiasm or trance. The heroic-adventurous attempt to adore existence as something delightful and great, and to surrender completely to beauty, is followed by the hollow feeling of bankruptcy and discouragement, a feeling that borders on morbidity. This state of affairs was brilliantly dramatized in Koheleth: "All is vanity" (Ecclesiastes 1:2). Boredom does not characterize the ethical experience but the aesthetic. This is what Adam and Eve found out after they ate from the Tree of Knowledge: "they opened their eyes and knew that they were naked" (Gen. 3:7), that their nude and senseless lives were full of absurdity and worthless.

Boredom is the admission of the meaninglessness of the aesthetic existence. Why? Simply because the aesthetic gesture is non-teleological. No vision awaiting realization addresses itself to Adam, no distance to be covered beckons to him. No promised land draws him on, impelling him to journey through desert sands and hot dunes. For Adam the morrow will not differ from the today, which, in turn, did not attain anything that had not been there yesterday. He does not travel from one position to another, heading toward a great destination, for he has none. The aesthetic experience is not a purposeful one; it is not eager to realize something; hence all the adventures and heroic poses come to naught. The aesthete looks back upon a past rich in experience but devoid of accomplishments, full of excitement but empty of meaning. Experience, however flamboyant and captivating, does not promote the idea of self-discovery, self-realization and self-redemption; experience thus withers like the flowers in the field. The excitement, though thrilling and rapturous, does not explain the rationale and goal of his existence, and it leaves him despondent and sad the morning after. Boredom is a feeling of disillusionment and teleological void.

Must beauty be deprived of all transcendental content and intentionality? If that is so, it is because, by definition, the awareness of beauty is closed in by finite, phenomenal and conditional nature. Maimonides named the aesthetic value judgment *mefursam*, conventional, and this term conveys the superficial nature of the aesthetic project. Yet this may not be the entire story. The contrary can be proposed, namely, that the aesthetic life is a mere representation of a rational world surrounding us, and of a naked experience of the new. Though the aesthetic, in itself, never ventures outside of immediacy and contiguity, it is more than that: it is an incessant search for the beyond, for a finer, better and purer existence which has been purged of the ugliness of ordinary, unredeemed existence. Judaism attempted a revolutionary undertaking: to ethicize the aesthetic experience, to raise it to a teleological level.

The next chapter examines the way in which Judaism attempted to redeem the aesthetic experience. This analysis will elucidate the manner in which the depth crisis precipitated by the despair of the aesthetic contributes to the need awareness that is vital for petitionary prayer. It will also lead us to the other essential components in prayer—thanksgiving and praise.

🥖 Exaltation of God and Redeeming the Aesthetic

Aesthetics and the Question of Purpose

We have defined the aesthetic in terms of an immediate, constant contact with reality at the qualitative, sensible level. While the cognitive and the ethical experiences point toward infinity, the aesthetic remains bounded in by finitude. It is rooted in the very temporal and conditioned existence of man and does not transcend the limits of here and now reality. The aesthetic performance is not anchored in any transcendental eternal sphere. It is a thoroughly this-worldly phenomenon, which lays no claims to the beyond. Reason and will avail themselves of the methods of abstraction, thereby utilizing the full freedom of unlimited action, beyond the concrete and sensible, reaching for an absolute set of values and for the sanction and guarantor of these laws governing human behavior. The aesthetic man, restricted by the sensuous and tangible, while his fantasy roves desperately along the formal surface of our existence cannot, at first glance, free himself from its moorings in sensibility and in perceived immediacy. If there is no color, there is no perception of beauty for the eye; if the universe is purged of sound, how then can the ear catch the sweet glorious music of the spheres? For the aesthetic, there is no beauty in the abstract, in thought alone.

The aesthetic occupation thus lacks purposiveness because of the absence of a transcendental motif, as opposed to both the intellectual and the ethical experiences. These are accompanied by the metaphysical awareness of transcendental ultimate truth and absolute ideals of the infinite mind and will, which lend legitimacy to our finite relative verities. When transcendence is absent, the telos cannot be envisioned, since the latter cannot be found in the realm which man controls, in the realm that is always accessible to him. Teleological thinking or acting is always a *metabasis els alios genos*—a leap into a different dimension, aspiration, or change of the very substance of existence, which is synonymous with the act of self-transcendence. Therefore, the ascription of purposiveness to the aesthetic act becomes a meaningless exercise.

Teleological activity is bound up with a distant vision, as the word *telos* signifies. Yet the destination can never be reached, it recedes with the hasty approach of the traveler. The nearer he comes, the farther it flees. Moses never entered the Promised Land; when he stood on Mount Nevo and gazed upon the land of dreams, it seemed to him to be more distant than at the time of the Exodus. The goal, both the cognitive and the moral, is always beyond the reach of the human being; it transcends endeavor. The impossibility of attainment is required to render an activity teleological. When realization is within reach, the term *telos* is inapplicable, since one is not then pursuing a transcendental objective.

If the aesthetic experience is to be cleansed and redeemed, it must express the transcendental yearning in man. Hence, it must always be encountered as a reflection of Divine beauty. It must direct the human eye toward the remote, infinite and exalted, suggest to the human being a nobler and sacred world, another order of existence. There is an eternal vision that beckons to the aesthete, which fascinates and pulls him towards unknown distances and uncharted lands. There is an ideal in the world of beauty as there is in the realm of ethics, an ideal that will never be completely attained. At this point we arrive at religious experience.

Let us clarify this thesis, about the relationship between the aesthetic and the teleological, by contrasting the aesthetic with the logos and the ethos—that is, the logical and the ethical. The latter are introspective, critical of themselves, always in doubt about the veracity of their pronouncements and perennially in search for some absolute and definitive premises. Hence, they are compelled to attach themselves to a transcendental order. The concrete order of things and values is ineffective in meeting the challenge of skepticism. Only the awareness of something else, different and outside of that which is directly converging on us, provides a safe anchor for the skeptical soul who is engaged in self-effacement and is self-negated. Whoever denies the transcendental relatedness of the cognitive or ethical act must accept an epistemological skepticism and a relativistic ethic and epistemology. This happened to the relativists and skeptics of antiquity, and also to those of modern times. Behind the doubt that assailed the minds of Hume, Mach, and Avenarius, is the fear of transcendental order and the prejudice of these philosophers against something that must be envisioned and not immediately sensed. Out of the fire of skepticism was born scientific thinking and civilized morality.

The same should be true of the aesthetic experience. Unfortunately, while man realized long ago that savagery must be eliminated from the logical realm and from the ethical, for otherwise mankind would never outgrow the habits of jungle and cave, the same standard was not applied to the aesthetic realm. Notwithstanding all philosophical theories, the aesthetic experience remained substantially unpurged, still full of its brute elements. Modern man continues to yield to the aesthetic with all the naivete and fervor of child fascinated by the sight of an electric train. This, despite the fact that the aesthetic value judgment needs sanction and legitimation just like the ethical and logical act. One must be able to reject certain phenomena even though they please the eye, as "false" manifestations of true beauty.

What is the story of the aesthete? Is he indeed immune to the type of doubting and questioning that have affected the logical and the ethical? Is he certain of the worth of his experience without having to place it in a realm that is above our finite existence? Or is he just as vulnerable to skepticism and relativism as the theoretician and ethicist, his consciousness abounding in questions and heresies about the importance and legitimacy of his own experiences? If the latter is true then the aesthete will have to contend with the problem of the ultimate worth of his experience. He will be compelled to wonder about the nature of beauty. In order to safeguard the unique character of his experience, he will be induced to seek the origin and the meaning of the beautiful. He will finally have to find the link between the sensuous experience and a suprasensory world. In other words: there will arise in his mind an aesthetic skepticism in the manner of epistemological and ethical skepticism.

Affinity of the Aesthetic and the Religious

The aesthetic experience has an affinity with the religious emotion. As a matter of fact, many a time it appears to us as if there is no conflict between the aesthetic and the religious, and that, on the contrary, instead of feuding they rather supplement each other. Religious worship, on the one hand, avails itself of artistic forms, and, on the other hand, art utilizes religious motifs and tries to express fundamentals of faith through aesthetic media.

Where is the link between the religious and the artistic experience? Where is the category that lends substance and form to both the aesthetic and religious gestures, to the perception of beauty and the experience of God? If such a category could be found, we would know how to transcendentalize the aesthetic performance, since such a supreme concept would bridge the gulf separating the Divine from the beautiful.

I believe that we may, in fact, speak of two categories that express both the aesthetic and the religious experience: the exalted and the heroic. Through these two primary forms of feeling a possibility is presented whereby to raise the aesthetic to the plane of transcendental. Let us here consider the category of the exalted.

The Exalted

The transition from the artistic to the religious is realized through the experience of the exalted. Beauty may be the typically aesthetic category that is experienced by the aesthete. The apprehension of beauty elevates the mind, cleanses the spirit, and, at least for a moment, ennobles the heart. A man feels overcome by the impact of beauty. However, he is not crushed by it; on the contrary, he recovers a sense of worthiness and dignity. This peculiar feeling flows from the encounter with the exalted or sublime, which reveals itself in beauty.

Exaltedness, by way of contrast, suggests to man the vision of something unique and great that is connected to witnessing the beautiful. It is basically a religious emotion. Exalted is God and exaltedness has the connotation of transcendence, being superior to, and elevated beyond and outside the human reach. In a word, it denotes infinity. Man cannot stop in his quest for perfection, for he will not be gratified, because there is something beyond the way station of sublimity and loftiness. Exalted is only the unattainable and inapproachable, and it can only be experienced if man is driven toward infinity itself. Truly, only God is exalted since only He is outside finite existence.

Judaism, which proclaimed the idea of transcendence, introduced exaltedness as a basic attribute of God. Isaiah relates of his vision that he saw God on a *"kisse ram ve-nissa,"* an exalted and high throne (Isaiah 6:1). Both terms express exaltedness and height beyond the created universe, that is to say transcendence. Isaiah portrays here the paradoxical vision of God. Under one aspect, He abides in the highest transcendental recesses, distant from and exalted above His creation; under another aspect, however, His train filled the temple—He resides in reality and is found in our immediate surroundings. The exclamation "Holy, holy, holy" (Isaiah 6:3) conveys also the experience of the exaltedness of God, of His separateness and remoteness, His infinity and transcendence.

Judaism achieved the discovery of aesthetic questioning through the idea of the exalted and transcendent using an epistemological viewpoint, in order to rehabilitate the aesthetic experience. As long as the aesthete is not troubled by the problem of whether his value judgment is correct, as long as his apprehension of the beautiful is uncritical, as long as complete surrender to the enthralling aesthetic vision is part of his daily routine, his experience will continue to have a desultory and unredeemed character. What is required is the awakening of the skeptic, the rise of a critique of the aesthetic judgment and beauty-appreciation. Through the emergence of doubt—the thought that everything experienced as beautiful is perhaps not beautiful at all—the catharsis of beauty is made possible. When the aesthete begins to wonder whether everything which is apprehended as beauty and as pleasant expresses indeed genuine beauty, when he thinks that the aesthetic act can be critically examined and its worth objectively ascertained, in a manner similar to our critical attitude toward the cognitive and ethical gestures, then beauty is redeemed.

There is a savageness in every human experience that is due to the unqualified acceptance of the data which we encounter. But it is not only the encounter with the beautiful and fascinating that yields an untamed experience. There is likewise a primitiveness, sometimes bordering on savagery, in the cognitive and ethical experience. The mythological and its interpretation of natural phenomena, or the Dionysian orgiastic cult, are excellent examples of brute theoretic and ethical interpretation. This sort of thinking and acting was purged by critical minds, by the skeptical approach.

But, as we stressed above, the feeling of the sublime and the lofty (exalted) is an inner motif of aesthetic experience. Therefore, the religious ecstatic vision and the aesthetic beholding meet at this juncture. At this point both experiences can commune with and influence each other. The aesthetic penetrates deeply into religious behavior and conversely, a religious theme may be incurred in the artistic.

In light of this thesis, we may state that God, for Judaism, is not only the source and root of truth and right, of fact and value, constituting the foundations of our theoretical and ethico-practical world, but also that He is the origin of beauty, of the delightful and the pleasant. God is not only omniscient (infinitely wise), not only full of grace, kindness and morality (infinitely good) but also sweet and lovely, fair and pleasant. God not only addresses Himself to man through the logos, by emanating wisdom and knowledge to the finite mind; not only through the ethos, revealing to natural man, driven by insensate desires and impulses, a great order of absolute values and ideals—but also through aesthesis—the immediate sensible apprehension of reality which is beautiful and grandiose. "The heavens tell the glory of God" (Ps. 19:2). In this enthusiastic exclamation, David does not refer to the mathematical precision of the movement of the planets and the propagation of light, but to the grandeur and splendor of the skies, to the innumerable natural phenomena whose charm and loveliness are beyond human imagination, reaching and saturating every fiber in creation. Is not the great hymn of *Borkhi nafshi* ("Let my soul bless") (Ps. 104:1) an outcry of the soul overfilled with beauty of nature, a joyful shout of a heart bursting with the great experience of a mighty and magnificent creation of God who clothes the world in *hod ve-hadar*, in magnificence and majesty?

"Taste and See"

One of Judaism's greatest achievements is that it ventured to accomplish the impossible, to meet God directly, not only via the abstract intellect or through the moral imperative, but also by employing sensuous media to apprehend Him.

This has been very ably expressed by Yehudah Halevi in his differentiation between the God of Abraham and the god of Aristotle (*Kuzari* 4:16ff). While the former is perceived, His presence felt, and the awareness of Him is a living and immediate one, the latter is only an abstraction and a metaphysical idea. In the passage from the *Kuzari* already cited in the first chapter, Halevi formulates a remarkable theory of religious sensuousness. He speaks of perceiving God! Only such a full, sensuous experience of God gratifies the God-thirsty soul and arouses passion and ecstatic love in man for the living God, for whom one is willing to incur martyrdom. Abstract experience does not inspire man. It is in the aesthesis, in the immediate beholding and perceiving of God that a voice is heard: "And His voice you heard from within the fire" (Deut. 5:21). "His glory and greatness" you have seen with the naked eye, His presence is sensed and felt with all its overpowering might, His splendor and beauty fascinates the sensuous man. One does not only think of God or comply with His will. One feels the touch of His hand and the warmth that His eyes radiate. "O taste and see that the Lord is good" (Ps. 34:9). In other words: experience God not through your facilities of abstracting conceptualization, which dismiss the immediate reality, but by tasting Him, as it were, by feeling Him right here and right now.

There is a contrast between indirect, inferential and abstract discovery of God and the immediate living encounter with Him. In the cognitive and the ethical act one approaches God by the process of deduction. There is no direct apprehension of the Creator. One arrives at the conclusion of governing cosmic intelligence by studying the universal drama and by reaching the fringes of the coherent causal nexus. In the ethical experience the process of inferring is considerably abbreviated, since the imperative pressure itself directs one's attention to God. Yet the conclusion, that the legitimacy of the norm requires relatedness to the absolute, dawns upon the ethical personality after long, careful study. The absolute of the logos and the ethos is more idea than fact, more mathematical boundary than reality, more postulate than living personal God, more abstraction than apprehension.

If we speak of experiencing God, and if by this we understand the ecstatic encounter of a man quivering with passion and tenseness, then one cannot consider the ethical or noetical act as capable of engendering such an experience. For the ethical and the cognitive, the rendezvous with the Creator is a quiet sedate one. There is, in fact, no actual meeting. A real encounter is never achieved by the scientist or the ethicist. For them, there is only, if we may use a metaphor of Yehudah Halevi, an exchange of epistles; the contact is established in an impersonal way, through correspondence.* The medium through which this type of contact is attained is the natural law and moral norm.

Only the aesthetic experience, if linked with the idea of the exalted, may bring man directly into contact with God, living, personal, and intimate. Only through coming in contact with the beautiful and exalted may one apprehend God instead of comprehending Him, feel the embrace of the Creator, and the warm breath of infinity hovering over a finite creation. The reason for immediacy and impact implicit in the aesthetic experience is its sensuous character.

This direct revelation of the Creator has always been explained by Judaism as a result of *kevod Elokim* (*majestas Dei*, the glory of God). Isaiah says "His glory fills the whole universe" (Isaiah 6:3). Glory of God expresses the aspect of revelation to

---

* Halevi's *Kuzari* (1:109) presents a parable about the king of India. The king is known only indirectly, through his communication. –*Ed.*

sensuous man: "The glory of God filled the tabernacle" (Ex. 40:34). "Blessed is the name of the *kavod* of His majesty forever and ever," as we recite immediately after the first verse of *Shema* (based on Ps. 72:19). While majesty alludes to the cosmic-dynamic role of God as creator and originator of the universe, the addition of *kavod* stresses the majesty element, a pure aesthetic phenomenon which fascinates and frightens man. *Majestas Dei* conveys the thought that absolute beauty rests in God, and that only He is the fountainhead out of which pulchritude, grace and loveliness flow into the world. The latter abounds in magnificent forms, in harmony, style and charm, because it was created in the likeness of its Master whose resplendent majesty and transcendent grace penetrate into every ramification of reality to the point of saturation.

"You are robed in *hod* and *hadar*, splendor and majesty" (Ps. 104:1). The God experience can also be immersed in aesthetic enthusiasm when man faces the grandeur. "When I see Your heavens, the work of Your fingers, moon and stars You fashioned" (Ps. 8:4); "How many are Your creatures O God, You have made them all with wisdom" (Ps. 104:24). The beauty of creation bears the majesty of God.

Thus, beauty has been linked up with transcendental and absolute Being and freed from the contingency of a volatile, passing and conditional world arrangement. God sanctions not only the true and the good but also the beautiful. It is delightful and fair because it reflects eternal glory and majesty. In beautiful things, the transcendental hint (to the something beyond) is inherent. Beauty is not hemmed in on all sides by the boundaries of finitude.

Man is fascinated by infinity not only because the transcendental order is the *ens realissimum* (pure being), or the *summum bonum* (absolute good), but because of *majestas Dei*. Divine beauty and glory captivate finite creation and the longing, the craving for the exalted sublime and the beautiful, is *ipso facto* a longing for God. Beauty as a motif in our lives must not be identified with the elusive and passing, but with the eternal and absolute. Religious passion, ecstatic love and Divine intoxication stem from the aesthetic awareness. Only beauty can be desired passionately, only loveliness can arouse enthusiasm and frenzy, and only the aesthetic experience may turn into an intoxicating drink, into a madness. Hence, Judaism has so glowingly spoken of the beloved *Dod* who is not only full of grace, but also graceful and fair, who is loved and desired, for whose embrace creation, like a young bride, craves and in whom it wants to rejoice. Is not *Shir ha-Shirim,* the Song of Songs, the great song of love, bordering on madness, for the beloved friend and bridegroom who is "fair and ruddy" (Song 5:10), for whom the maidens feel passion and indomitable desire?

It is not a coincidence that Judaism, in describing the relationship between man and God, has taken advantage of a very rich reservoir of sexual symbolism, similes and metaphors. The erotic love fans out in all directions reaching infinity itself. Judaism did not discriminate between *eros* (wordly love) and *agape* (purely spiritual love) as the Christian mystics did, but set up as a model of love of God, the unredeemed passion—not the spiritual, sublimated adoration. Maimonides, the intellectual aristocrat, could not forgo this imagery, however primeval, yet true. Maimonides glorified abstract scientific-philosophical thinking, as the *Guide* proclaims solemnly that only through such exact comprehension may one witness the absolute truth of Divine existence. Here we come across a basic contradiction in the Maimonidean worldview. In *Mishneh Torah* (*Hilkhot Yesodei ha-Torah* 2:2) he employed the aesthetic approach, when he stated that contemplating God's works and creatures leads man to love Him, and quoted David's psalm: "my soul thirsteth for God for the living God" (Ps. 42:3). Maimonides speaks of contemplation and wisdom. Yet the epithets he uses in describing the agitated mind that encounters the wondrous works are borrowed from the aesthetic experience. Elsewhere (*Hilkhot Teshuvah* 10:3), he compares man's love of God to a love-sick individual whose mind is at no time free of his passion for a particular woman, the thought of her filling his heart, quoting the verse "For I am sick with love (Song 2:5). *Shir Hashirim* is indeed an allegory descriptive of this love. This ecstatic love is born not out of a philosophical abstraction or ethical excellence but out of aesthetic beholding and apprehension. Only the senses can intoxicate man to such an extent, not the logos or the ethos. If one should love God with his whole heart and soul, the vision of God he beholds must be enveloped in beauty. God fascinates and charms, beckons and whispers like the fairest of lovers. Man, by placing beauty in the true perspective, as a reflection of Divine majestic glory, participates in God's majesty, which in turn bestows upon him high dignity.

Prayer and Religious Immediacy

In fact, prayer must be based upon aesthesis, upon religious immediacy and sensuousness. We emphasized at the outset that prayer, which is basically a dialogue between God and man, thus supplanting prophecy, attains communal relationship between Creator and creation. Community existence is only possible if both parties joining into this type of fellowship encounter each other as real personalities whose presence is immediately felt and acknowledged.

The I and the Thou that make up the community are not abstractions. Relationships between abstract entities are only formal, mathematical: hence they cannot create community-bonds and commitments. A community of existence can only emerge when there is an encounter at the concrete level of sensuous portraiture, realizing the presence of the parties committed to a common destiny. The persons involved in a communal venture must experience each other. Only the feeling of closeness can promote community awareness. Otherwise, companionship would be a meaningless word.

When we speak of religious sensuousness we must note carefully that there are many senses to this term. Religious sensuousness may denote actual sensuous representation of religious material, vision and imagery, including definite portrayal of the transcendental order. We should not look askance at visionary mystics who actually see God. Regardless of psychologistic interpretations of these images, they nurture the God-hungry soul and express an experience that is too rich and too dynamic to be satisfied with trite philosophical terms. I could never feel sympathy for Maimonides' horror at religious-sensuous portrayal.

On the other hand, religious sensibility may manifest itself, not in bold pictorial representation, but in experiential immediacy. Contact is established with the Almighty in the abyss of a warm heart, in a love-sick soul, in the experience of the invisible, in the richness of the inner life, in being aware of something supernal, great, awesome and beautiful, although this "something" is neither seen nor heard. However devoid of sensuous material this feeling is, it is still an immediate reality, whose impact upon the religious person is enormous. In a word, the aesthetic experience of God, whether constructed of impressions and sensations drawn from our daily life, where man is engrossed in images and psychophysical sensuous processes, or consisting of ecstatic emotions, in the throbbing of the heart and the longing of the soul, is the basis of the community of God and man.

It is impossible to imagine prayer without, at the time, feeling the nearness and greatness of the Creator, His absolute justice, His fatherly concern with human affairs, His anger and wrath caused by unjust deeds. When we bow in prayer, we must experience His soothing hand and the infinite love and mercy for His creatures. We cling to Him as a living God, not as an idea, as abstract Being. We are in His company and are certain of His sympathy. There is in prayer an experience of emotions which can only be produced by direct contact with God.

Hymn and Adoration

Let us investigate the connection between prayer and the problem of purposiveness tied to the aesthetic experience. At this point, we must turn to the prologue of all prayer in our liturgy, hymnal praise. What does the hymn mean as an expression of the religious state of mind? It signifies a rise of religious emotion. When the religious temperament is aroused, the soul is stirred and the experience becomes tempestuous. Under the impact of such an inner wave of rapture, man begins to adore God and to sing a hymn to Him. Usually, as I indicated above, it is a spontaneous uttering of a powerful and deep stirring of the human personality. A passionate affection, and not an abstract faith, expresses itself in hymns. As such, the hymn is an expression of an intoxicated and excited mind, and is therefore a pure aesthetic phenomenon. Man admires beauty in all its manifestations. This admiration cannot be contained in the subjective, mute, inner world of man; hence it tries to break into the external world of movement through tangible sensation. It expresses itself in primitive religion through absurd choreographic rites; and in civilized religion—in the singing of hymns.

Religious passion and excitement make a strenuous effort to surpass their common limits of inwardness, and to convert themselves into action. However, all this is purely an aesthetic performance. One neither essentially admires goodness, nor adores intellectual greatness. Of course, the logos and ethos may become objects of great beauty, and as such arouse human admiration with their grandeur and grace. Yet, whatever is adored is clothed in beauty. The ethical and cognitive experiences are, in their essence, emotionally mute and they are subject to uncontrollable compulsions. Only beauty is beholden in rapture.

Praise and Thanksgiving

The aesthetic apprehension is loud and may often pass into a tumultuous state of mind. *Birkot ha-shevah*, the blessings of praise which one pronounces over certain aesthetic experiences, redeem them from crudity and finite transience. The aesthetic is raised to a world of eternal beauty in God, to *kevod malkhuto (majestas Dei)*. Thus, beauty finds its salvation in the One who is both root and ultimate end of all aspirations and deeds. The aesthete becomes conscious of the transcendental character of this particular experience of desire. He suddenly gains insight into his craving for beauty, which is nothing but the eternal longing for eternal noumenal Being.

Thus the Absolute reveals itself not only to the metaphysician but also to the gazer upon beauty. An Absolute, which abides beyond volatile appearances beckons, not only to the ethicist but also to the *homo aesthesis*. *Birkot ha-shevah* perform the feat of relating the beautiful to the eternal, truthful and good. Each aesthetic impression of creation is focused *ipso facto* upon the Creator.

The term *shirah* (song) in the Halakhah signifies the externalization of aesthetic experience, the outpouring of a grateful soul seething with longing and yearning for the beloved who is lovely and full of grace. "This is my God and I will adore Him" (Ex. 15:2) is the motto of the *shirah*. God is extolled and adored because He is beautiful.

Both the extolling and thanksgiving hymn are expressions of the aesthetic experience. There is a basic difference between praise and thanksgiving. The former expresses the glory of God, His might and majesty. The cosmic drama impresses us with its orderliness and reverence. These emotions are represented by adoration of the Author of this beautiful awe-inspiring drama. Singing of praise is the central part of the adoration. In this form of worship, God is experienced ecstatically as the artist and master whose creation abounds in grace and loveliness. The hymn often expresses what Otto called the numinous, the unknown, the strange, the mysterious that glimmers in boundless uniformity, and in the variety of creation, in every corner and nook before which man stands in awe-struck amazement, in divine rapture. The hymn reaches its most solemn and powerful note in the *Kedushah* (trishagion), the song of the Seraphim: "Holy, holy, holy" (Isaiah 6:3).

The beauty of God is experienced as holiness, as the *mysterium magnum*, ineffable and unattainable, awesome and holy (*nora ve-kadosh*), as something that transcends everything comprehensible and speakable, which makes one tremble and also experience bliss. Beauty and paradox merge—He is both remote and so near, awesome and lovely, fascinating and daunting, majestic and tender, comforting and frightening, familiar and alien, the beyond of creation and its very essence. He is everywhere and yet nowhere, in all and still transcendent to everything. You find Him in both growth and decay, in creation and destruction, He is the principle of life and the master of death. He is mystery from which you desire to flee and yet you try to cling to it. This unknown is extolled and adored by angels and mortals alike. The greatest vision of beauty occurs when man encounters the *Kadosh* (the Holy) who can neither be seen nor approached nor controlled and yet is experienced as the root of everything.

The thanksgiving service is also an aesthetic performance, yet it differs in a major aspect from the hymn. God in the thanksgiving hymn is proclaimed primarily as good, as helping, giving and loving, as charitable and full of grace and mercy. We declare His will to be the abode of ethical and moral law, His deed a continuing process of realization of His infinite good. The vision of the kind God engenders a feeling of gratitude and indebtedness that finds expression in a hymn. In short, in the thanksgiving hymn we sing of God's *hesed* (lovingkindness). Good becomes an aesthetic value; it turns into beauty. We experience the moral law not so much as an imperative but as something beautiful. Its binding power is supplanted with a quality of fascination; the decision, by desire; surrender by merger. Whenever this happens the gratitude, which is, at one level, no more than a feeling of expedience, turns into enthusiasm, and indebtedness into rapturous love. God is good and therefore beautiful. This sort of beauty is not identical with majesty, but it does manifest itself in grandeur and vastness, in the powerful drama of the creation. It emerges as *caritas* or *amor Dei*.

Experiencing the infinite goodness of God as beautiful means to encounter Him, not as a mystery, defying all rules of orderliness, eluding the grasp of the necessary and lawful and harmonious. He is no longer the strange, alien, numinous God who makes the worshipper shudder, wonder-struck in the presence-absence of the unknown and mysterious. On the contrary, *caritas Dei* inspires, ennobles, and befriends man. God is known to and intimate with him. There is no attempt to flee Him, since the experience is not numinous; it is not "wholly other," to use Otto's characterization of the numinous. Man tries to imitate God, walk in His ways and participate in His *caritas*. Of course, God's charity is infinite and our finite mind can only understand an infinitesimal portion of His goodness. Yet the moral infinity of God, however suprarational and distant from us, is not frightening or awe-inspiring, but on the contrary, beckons to us and invokes in us the desire for imitation and merger. We do not stand aghast in the presence of the numen when we sing to God a thanksgiving hymn and adore His goodness and His infinite might and grace.

Beauty, majesty, in themselves, arouse in us emotions of dread and horror (*pahad*); we shudder: "Serve God in fear; rejoice in trembling" (Ps. 2:11). The unknown and mysterious looms on the far horizons of one's visionary awareness. Yet, when the good is apprehended as the beautiful, it arouses emotions of a different kind—craving for communion and contact, a desire for sharing in God's charitable works and for following His laws and guidance. The moments of daunting, the impulse of fleeing in trembling and awe are completely missing from the experience of the infinite good. On the contrary, the good allures, not with its strangeness and otherness, but with its familiar aspects. In this way, the good appeals to us, inviting us to make it our own. Instead of bewildering, it fascinates us. It engenders a feeling of felicity and love; it soothes our excited emotions and stills the suffering of a ravaged heart. What we are aware of is not something uncanny, alien, which is beyond the sphere of the orderly, the lawful and the normal, and which astounds us, but of something close to and intimately related to us, which we try to acquire and take possession, to which our soul responds and clings passionately. This something is not beyond the grasp of order and nomos but on the contrary their full realization and representation.

The Structure of the Hymns: An Analysis of Psalms 103 and 104

The typical hymnal song includes the following motifs:

First, that God is Creator of the world and also its master: "His is the sea and He created it, and the dry land is formed by His Hands" (Ps. 95:5). Because the natural is grandiose, mighty and orderly, it bears witness to the absolute beauty of the august Creator Whose majesty is reflected on us.

Second, that man, encountering the cosmic drama, is aware of his metaphysical worthlessness and vanity. Psalm 90 and Psalm 8 are representative of this theme. He is, at the same time, overcome by an indomitable longing for God. Even though he feels his helplessness and wretchedness, he still tries to commune with the Creator.

Lastly, that the Creator is not only omnipotent, omniscient, great and magnificent but unknown and unknowable.

These are the main patterns of our liturgical hymns. Our liturgical literature contains both the extolling and the thanksgiving hymns. As the two most exquisite hymns representing both kinds we may introduce the two psalms, beginning with *Borkhi nafshi* (103, 104), and examine them in detail. The first psalm expresses thanks to the Creator. The refrain "Let my soul bless God" is to be understood in the sense of offering thanks to God. In the second psalm David expresses not thanks but praise; he extols God and the phrase "Let my soul bless God" means that my soul praises Him.

In the thanksgiving psalm, David sees in God the loving Father, the kind Healer, the benevolent Forgiver, the God of mercy, long sufferance and endless grace. A note of familiarity and intimacy is quite discernible in the rhythmic flow of David's phrases. The psalm is calm, descriptive and restrained in its praise and adoration. The tones are muted, the metaphors simple and unpretentious. There is, at least in the first 18 verses, no mention of the numinous. Man, although transient and lonely, does not shudder in His presence. The reverse is true. He finds peace and happiness in the Almighty, since He is his loving Father and Caretaker.

By comparison with this chapter, the following hymn of praise strikes us with its powerful tones: "You have garbed Yourself in *hod* and *hadar*; wrapped in light like a dress..." (104:1-2). Here is an enraptured, triumphant and ecstatic hymn to Him whose is the magnificence and glory, breaking through the hushed sounds of the foregoing chapter, and converging upon us with its fully unfolded splendor. Of course, Psalm 104 gives a manifold expression to this experience of *majestas Dei*. We encounter in it rise and fall, an astounding frequency of emotions. It strikes out with thrilling passages and after a while subsides into a descriptive narration. Yet, the psalmist is not able to restrain his feelings for very long and suddenly an outcry of a soul agitated and transported with a unique ravishment echoes again through the psalm: "How many are Your creatures O God, You have made them all with wisdom..." (v. 24). The calm descriptive whisper swells again to a great hymn of adoration.

It is interesting that the numinous element comes to the fore at the outset and at the conclusion of the hymns. As a matter of fact, the latter part of Psalm 103, forming the transitional link between the thanksgiving and the extolling hymns, strikes a numinous note: "Man's days are like grass" (103:15ff). The numen expresses itself in an admission of impotence, collapse, futility of man's undertakings, and his bankruptcy. This creature awareness is contrasted with the eternity and infinite grace and power of God: "the *hesed* (lovingkindness) of God everlasting" (17).

From this perspective, David begins to praise God, the numinous, the omniscient, the omnipotent, the Ruler who with all His compelling power, which pervades the whole creation, remains *Deus absconditus*: unique, incomprehensible and mysterious. David stresses the power of God more than any other attribute. However, the unlimited power of God makes us shudder before Him and dread Him. The encounter with infinite power is an overwhelming experience; God appears as austere, stern, before Whom man is just dust and ashes and abhorrent to himself.

The numinous epilogue to the thanksgiving Psalm 103 serves as the introduction to the great hymn of Psalm 104, which sings to the God of majesty and beauty. This hymn, in turn, displays the numinous element at the very beginning: "God Thou art extolled, You have garbed Yourself in magnificence and majesty (*hod ve-hadar*)" (104:1). God is not accessible; He is infinite, distant and abides in absolute seclusion (v. 3).

These parallels express the paradoxical nature of God's actions. He rides on the cloud and moves upon the wings of the wind. There is numb amazement at the glory of God, His movements and actions: "He makes His messengers winds; his servants flaming fire" (v. 4). Yet, the two significant aspects of the numinous emerge in the psalm when David develops what, at first glance, are contradictory ideas: "God rejoices in His works. He looks upon the earth and it trembles" (31-32). For God is both the creator and destroyer. His presence at times soothes and quiets man, imparts to him certainty and joy. His companionship is life itself. God is our shepherd and friend, supporting and comforting (Ps. 23). Yet, sometimes His emergence from His transcendental mysterious recesses spells catastrophe for a frail and weak creation. The numinous presence crushes man with its impact:

> Then the earth shook and trembled; the foundations also of the hills moved and were shaken because He was wroth. There went up a smoke out of His nostrils and fire out of His mouth devoured: coals were kindled by it (Ps. 18:8-9).

To come close to God, according to this verse, is tantamount to self-effacement. Contact with Him undermines the very existence of man. The great fire engulfs the little candle. Infinity is not only the womb from which finitude emerges but also the bottomless abyss into which it plunges in its quest for the unattainable. Man seeks, in vain, to hide: "Enter into the rock and hide there in the dust for fear of the Lord and for the glory of His majesty" (Isaiah 2:19).

This numinous pardox is very characteristic of our religious consciousness. God is not only a sustaining, merciful, and loving Creator and Father, but also a negating and devastating power Who mercilessly extinguishes life and existence. His countenance is radiant with beatitude. "I shall behold Your face in righteousness. I shall be satisfied when I awake with Your likeness" (Ps. 17:15). At the same time, however, no one may see His face, for a mere glance at God's countenance results in instantaneous termination of one's life, "for man cannot see Me and live" (Ex. 33:20).

The *numen praesens* (the presence of God) is dreadful and the least encounter with Him dooms man to extinction. This experience, too, is an intrinsic part of our God-awareness. The word *havayah* has a twofold connotation: creating, constituting, calling something into being, and also negating, annihilating, undermining. (For the latter meaning, see Ex. 9:3: "the hand of God devastates (*hoyah*)" Egypt's cattle.) Religious fear, expressing itself in the apprehension of a punitive action on the part of Deity with regard to man the sinner, is rooted in the daunting moment within the God experience. A religion accepting love as the sole medium through which God addresses Himself to man is guilty of one-sidedness. God is both the lover and the stern judge, the sustaining and destroying power. Man must experience this peculiar mystery of the Creator-Annihilator, the moment of stern justice and wrath (*haron af*). Encountering God the awesome, the finite is repelled by infinity. And man, fleeing to God, the alone clinging to the Alone, is thrown back into the dreariness of solitude.

Yet our psalm emphasizes another element in our religious experience: *numen absens* (the absence of God). Here man is daunted and shocked not by the Divine presence, but by something else. Man is awe-struck by God's absence. God befriends man and animal, plays with, cares for and caresses them lovingly. Creatures feel close to Him. Faith in Him as a companion and undismayed trust in His word are suddenly disrupted when God hides His face and disappears from their midst, leaving behind nothingness and a silent desert. Man is shattered and stunned, perplexed and frightened. These unpredictable hidings of the face, the withdrawals on the part of God, are felt in awe and amazement. The Divine, to use a phrase of F. W. Robertson, many a time evaporates from creation like the morning dew, and when God, Who just touched our head tenderly is gone, we feel forlorn and small and worthless: "You hide Your face, they are confused" (v. 29). The feeling of His absence is the great *mysterium tremedum*: Man stands in fear and tremor before the *numen absens* and implores Him to return: "You send forth Your spirit, they are created; You renew the face of the earth" (v. 30).

Psalm 103 concludes with a triumphant hymn to the Unknown. Psalm 104 ends with an ethical motif. This is typical of the interaction between the aesthetic and the ethical in Judaism. Yet we have uncovered in these great hymns the disturbing notes of the numinous presence and the baffling experience of Divine absence. God is experienced not only as a friend but as antagonist as well. This paradoxical situation requires our further attention. It will be the theme of the next chapter.

❧ The Absence of God and the Community of Prayer

The Struggle With God

In our earlier analysis we have already encountered God as *numen praesens*—a benevolent presence—and as *numen absens*—an experience of danger and menace. He wrestled with Jacob in the darkness of the night. He met Moses at the inn and wanted to destroy him. Yet, both Jacob and Moses emerged from this struggle stronger and happier than before. Out of the dreadful night of numinous experience comes forth a blessing, a great feeling of felicity. The religious experience does not always free man from care and pain, as many religious leaders assert. The believer is not always without sorrow and at peace with himself and the world. We find him quite often torn by inner conflicts and doubts, groping in the dark, wrestling with his own conscience and convictions. The transcendental experience weighs heavily upon him. He tries to cast it off and rid himself of that great burden, under whose impact he walks humbly and slavishly, committed to duties that he dislikes, to restraints and sacrifices that he resents, without being able to lift his head in full dignity and to regain his freedom and independence of living.

To be religious is not to be confused with living at ease, with unruffled calmness and inner peace. On the contrary, the religious life is fraught with emotional strife, intellectual tensions which ravel and fray its harmony. The religious experience not only warms, but also chills with horror. The religious is not only swayed by joy, but also by sadness and pain. All the modern theories about the healing function of religion see only one phase of the religious experience, the sublimated one. At the primeval stage, the experience is marked by the chill and rigor of the unknown. Only when man lives through the great encounter with the unknown in the night of doubt, suffering incessant dread and depression, does he experience the daybreak of a cheerful faith, full of promise of delivery and bliss. Moreover, in the very experience of doom and horror there is an undertone of joy. In the hopeless pain of surrender, in the tragedy of wrestling with the mysterious *ish* (the man who wrestled with Jacob in the night) the contours of a great and joyful drama of existence are discernable.

The numinous element is important because it lends greatness to the religious experience; it deepens the human awareness of the existential and metaphysical antinomies that his nature involves and brings his historical destiny into a sharp focus. Therefore, the contrast of tragedy and cheer, the opposition of despair and joy that is so characteristic of the religious life. It brings the most profound of human experiences, the religious feeling, to full life and fruition.

The Struggle With the Absence of God

Judaism holds fast to the belief that God reveals Himself through two media—the cosmic-natural and the historical-axiological. Both the physical universe and the spiritual one are permeated with the glory of God. Creation stands for the cosmic revelation while prophetic revelation (in both forms, apocalyptic and intuitive) represents the vision of God against the historical order. The numinous approach, which we have already encountered, and the kerygmatic approach, which stresses man's participation in the Divine mission, are both typical of the religious experience. Therefore, they are integral parts of Divine revelation at *both* levels—the cosmic and the historical.

Let us examine the opposition of dread and longing of mystery, on the one hand, and familiarity, on the other hand, as it is experienced on both planes. At the cosmic level the numinous manifests itself in two spheres.

First, the numinous is apprehended in the seemingly mechanical arrangement of cosmic occurrence. Events are connected by automatic forces, which express themselves in mathematical relationships. *Prima facie* this approach does not disclose any governing intelligence in nature, no power which intervenes at times in the monotony of creation, and which adapts brute meaningless forces to a higher will. Causality itself, as formulated in the mechanistic interpretation of the cosmic process, manifests nothing but senselessness and the absence of plan and pattern.

The experience of *numen absens* (the numinous experienced as an absence) in the cosmic process has been intensified in modern times with the dizzying success of scientific achievements and technological conquests. The machine, whose major performance is an assembly of coordinated subfunctions, has become the cornerstone of our world philosophy and has shut out the vision of God. Not always do the heavens proclaim the glory of God. Instead, man encounters a seemingly unresponsive attitude on the part of the cosmic forces towards man, his needs and his aspirations. Man feels a grisly emptiness and chilling cruelty pervading the uncharted lanes of the universe; encumbering, vast, almost endless distances suggest to man the stillness, darkness and insensation of Being which is intimately knit with non-being. Nature is cool, mechanical and devoid of meaning; man, searching for salvation, is a tragi-comical figure crying out to a mute insensible environment, which does not share his troubles and suffering.

In vast, dark stretches of empty space matter is born and destroyed, galaxies spring into being and disappear by force of inner necessity, impelled by nonsensical laws. It appears as if the "firmament over our heads is like the color of terrible crystal" (Ezekiel 1:22). Man prays to the hidden God: Please reveal Thyself to me; show me a sign that Thou art here and there, that the universe is not a still desert, where the accidental event reigns supreme. Not always, however, does he receive an answer to his fervent prayers. Man seeks God in nature and he cannot find: "Let me rise and wander in the town; have you seen Him whom my soul loves?" (Song 3:2).

This feeling stems from the depths of our religious consciousness whenever we encounter stupendous nature, ruthless and inconsiderate toward man. The fact of natural catastrophes, disease, starvation and physical pain bears witness to the loneliness and helplessness of man amidst strange surroundings and his estrangement from God who hides His face from him.

Second, in the historical realm, the numinous comes to expression when man suddenly becomes aware of the unreasonableness of historical occurrence. Instead of advancing toward the realization of a great destiny, history recedes, sweeping men and events towards their primeval beginning and savagery.

The parallelism between the historical and cosmic process is striking. The encounter with unreasonableness occurs in both realms. There is solemnity, fullness and overabundance of meaning in nature, when man delights in all the nuances of the tone and tempo of life, when he enjoys the world surrounding him, because wherever he turns he finds God. There is also grandeur and magnificence in history, when man feels secure in his position as participant in the historical drama, when events are molded in a way that points towards a distant ultimate end, sought passionately by man. However, this kerygmatic experience is more often an exception than a rule in history. Many a time man wonders whether or not God cares to intervene on his behalf. The tragic search for God, Who hides His face, is the great undertaking of man, and it frequently ends in despair and resignation.

The Bible abounds in the complaints and pleas of the prophets who, even as they were committed to God and had unshakable faith in Him, were frightened by His absence from their midst. They were terrified by thoughts of the void, the weird darkness and chaos preceding creation, and dismayed by prayers unheard, and sacrifices rejected, and martyrdom incurred seemingly in vain by the just and righteous. The prophet shudders, seeing a world ruled by inhumanity and brutality.

The prophet encounters the numinous absence of God with despair and fear. Absolute wondrousness and dismay, which decry all intellectual attempts to understand, cry out of these exclamations. Yet, each chapter closes with an optimistic cheerful note of hope and redemption. Habakuk 3 offers an excellent example of this characteristic. In this song the numinous turns kerygmatic; the religious experience runs from one pole to another. The conclusion stands sharply against the despondent and depressive tone at the beginning. But this change is not arbitrary. It is rooted in the very essence of the religious experience.

The experience of the *numen absens*, of an empty world, at a cosmic and historical level, is shattering. And not only the stately joy of faith and closeness to the Infinite, but also the sadness and gloom of metaphysical solitude and existential void flow from a religious fountainhead. The experience of a deserted, dreary world must not be confused with agnosticism or Greek mythological fatalism. It is the religious emotion at its best. Solitary man, who dreads the unknown and who feels lost in a boundless universe, does not fall prey to his fearful experiences, however distressing the latter might prove to be. He shows remarkable resilience. Therefore, he is not to be categorized by the ancient Greek tragedy, where human action is completely compulsive, where freedom of decision and initiative are an absurdity, and man just a withered leaf carried along by a raging, absurd storm. In Judaism, the numinous experience is a prologue to redemption—man hopes to free himself finally from the dreadful, and to march forward towards beatitude and bliss. Eschatology is the final destination of the religious experience, and an eschatological experience means a redeemed one, when the now unknown will appear in our midst as an old friend and acquaintance, when man will see God, feel His presence, and enjoy Him continuously, when the curtain of the numinous will be raised. Yet, eschatology is placed outside the historic-cosmic circle. As long as our existence is fenced in by the historic and the natural—our experience of God is a dual one.

The Experience of Loneliness

At this point, we come face to face with another aspect of the human depth crisis—the loneliness of man in the universe. He is thrown into a world that has neither regard nor understanding for his singular role. He is a tiny speck, floating in a vast sea of brute thinghood and mechanical existence. The other intelligent Being in Whom he may find sympathy and concern is distant and invisible, hiding beyond the cloud of mystery and transcendence. The numinous experience of God casts its shadow upon the surroundings of man. If God is absent from the immediate end, then man is trapped. When he lifts his eyes he sees only dreary spaces and emptiness. "A roaring sea moves toward Him, darkness engulfs him" (Isaiah 5:30).

This loneliness crisis of the human being differs from the boredom crisis which we discussed earlier. While boredom is the result of the absence of meaningful, teleological action in human life, loneliness flows from the awareness of drifting, a lack of roots and anchorage. One is bored because he does not envision something distant in prospect. He is lonely because he cannot see something far off in retrospect. Koheleth was ignorant of his destiny, Job of his origin. The feeling of loneliness is synonymous with uprootedness. A withered leaf driven by the cold autumn wind is lonely.

Even the experience of the beautiful and the graceful, as we discussed above, becomes boring. It leaves man with a feeling of non-accomplishment. In order to free himself from this awareness, he must redeem the experience of the beautiful by disentangling it from the transient and illusory, from the apprehension of something which is given, and by relating it to something which is beyond the creature-datum, to something that transcends the present, to the exalted, inapproachable and unknown. He does so by relating the aesthetic to the numinous.

But the experience of loneliness cannot be resoved in this way. To encounter the unknown, the *numen absens*, means to experience the dreadful feeling of loneliness, of a solitary and desolate existence, a creature fallen away from the Creator and the Sustainer. It is to be an I who cannot address himself to the Thou. The I who is alone drifts along endless stretches. Man cannot unburden himself of the numinous, since this mystery-awareness is an integral part of his religious experience.

This experience, from which man cannot disengage himself, forms the backdrop against which the outlines and contours of prayer become discernible. The feeling of loneliness impels man to search for companionship. Man is, as Aristotle said, a social animal; hence he is always eager to share his experiences with others, to live a communal life in order to redeem himself from the dreadful feeling of being alone. Loneliness, however, is rooted in the experience of the *numen absens*. Therefore, the fear of estrangement from Being, and the drive to tie the existence of the I with that of the Thou, cannot be reduced merely to a social-psychological dimension. Rather it stems from the ontic-awareness of man.

Hence, the formation of accidental friendships at a finite level does not give comfort to a lonely soul. The craving for love must be gratified at the plane of the God-man encounter. Only through such a meeting, at which the finite creature addresses itself to the Creator, is an I-Thou relationship established, thus providing man with something that he could not attain in his social life, namely, the awareness of togetherness and community existence. The best medium through which such a paradoxical fellowship is achieved is the prayer-dialogue.

In prayer, man tries to break through the unknown to the kerygmatic and to attain contact with the Creator, to convert tenseness into intimacy, strangeness into acquaintance. Judaism wants him to take courage and address himself to God, and by boldly approaching Him—the Infallible and Unknowable—to lift the veil and dreadful mystery of the numen. When this takes place, man finds the unknown to be an old friend; in the numen he discovers the intimately Known, radiating warmth and love. Through prayer, man accomplishes the impossible: the transformation of the numinous into the kerygamatic, of fear into love and of absence into presence. Thus when prayer is born, a community is established and man finds himself no longer lonely, forlorn; there are two lonely beings who have sought and found each other. This relation is not a functional but an existential one.

From Loneliness to Community

What is the method employed by man to convert a numinous feeling into a community experience?

At the historical level, the experience of fellowship flows from the awareness of our unique charismatic quality and our covenantal relationship to Him. In spite of His frequent, frightening withdrawals from our midst, He cannot, on juridic grounds, forsake us, because He has committed Himself to our ancestors and entered into a contractual relationship with them, and this covenantal obligation cannot be rescinded. Community existence has been promised to us and in God's word we take refuge.

The relationship of the *Avot* (Patriarchs) to the Creator can be characterized as a composite experience. Strangeness and marvel intermingle with familiarity and fellowship. There were moments when they experienced apocalyptic dread and fear as, for instance, in that mysterious twilight when Abraham was awestruck (Gen. 15). Indeed, the very promise made to Abraham with respect to the Land of Canaan was contingent upon a numinous historical experience. Abraham's children would not have inherited the land if they had not paid the high price of living for centuries in slavery, suffering the horrors of brutality in the land of Egypt: "Know that your seed will be strangers in a land that is not theirs; they will be subjugated and oppressed..." (Gen. 15:13).

We witness similar intermittent numinous experiences in the *Akedah* (the binding of Isaac), in Jacob's dream, in the tragic controversy between Joseph and his brothers, among other episodes. Yet the numinous is always translated into the kerygmatic, which is, to the Fathers, the genuine feeling, and which overcomes the state of amazement in the presence of the Almighty and its paradoxical expression in terms of flight and emotional chaos. Whatever transpired, however terrible the experience, the *Avot* always acted as if avowing themselves freely and deliberately to be overpowered, not as if they were merely crushed and vanquished by some strange power that could not be resisted. They discovered the formula that helps man to translate his numinous experience into a kerygmatic experience, namely the acceptance of the numinous authority, truly, wholeheartedly and with conviction, the result of which is the easing of the mind and dispelling of inner fear and anxiety.

They submitted to the numen, not under constraint, as an expression of impotence and helplessness in the face of overwhelming experience, but out of conviction and free choice. They considered the dreadful and mysterious encounter to be a summons to man, not to yield to something unknown, but to interpret the unknown in terms of a great experience, one that enriches and purifies man. That is why one recites a blessing for evil occurrences just as one thanks God for good tidings (Mishnah *Berakhot* 9:2; *Hilkhot Berakhot* 10:3).

If the approach to the numinous is molded in categories of free acceptance, then the gap separating the kerygmatic from the numen is closed. At this point the idea of repentance emerges. According to the Halakhah, the latter is indissolubly intertwined with crises, with the *numen absens* experience of *tsarah*: "When you are in distress... you shall repent unto your God" (Deut. 4:30). The link between suffering and repentance is to be found in the peculiar interpretation of the numinous. The encounter with the numinous gives birth to a cathartic, purifying and ennobling state of mind, if it is freely and thoughtfully experienced. The unworthiness of the finite in contrast to the Almighty is extenuated through the numinous, and man subsequently finds it easier to approach God and to be intimate with Him. God does not admit man to Himself unless he has gone through the experience of atonement. This idea that the finite unworthy person experiences catharsis through the acceptance of suffering is illustrated in Abraham's encounter with the numinous (to which we alluded before) when he is told that his seed will be oppressed in a foreign land. The numinous is the proper medium for realizing this postulate of atonement.

It is a prerequisite for greatness to experience the numinous in all its strangeness and alienness, inconsiderateness and non-responsiveness. To repeat: one must not surrender to the numinous as to a superior power that silences all opposition. Rather, one must make a supreme effort to assimilate it into one's total existential experience, to interpret it and to search for the message hidden in something paradoxical and alien, a message which may change a man's entire outlook on the world and himself. No wonder that *tefillah* is the response of man to the numinous whenever he encounters it. The reason is that the function of *tefillah* is to convert a strange and incomprehensible relationship into friendship and comradeship.

That is why *tefillah* begins by referring to the God of Abraham, Isaac and Jacob. It is because our fathers displayed the ability to interpret the numinous in terms of a great kerygma. They took the absolute inconceivability (Otto's term) of the great mysterious experience and found in it an inexpressible order, positive and sustaining. Out of utter despair emerges the great message. Whenever man is swept into the abyss, whenever meaninglessness seems to have deflated purposiveness and sense, man rises up, striding vigorously over the mystery toward the revelation of a message.

From Community to Law

How did the *Avot*, the Fathers, achieve their triumph over fear and the awareness of nothingness? The answer to this question must be sought in the normative character of the God-experience; that is to say, in the parallelism prevailing between the norm implied in God's encounter with man, and the Divine revelation through the cosmos. Halakhah never acquiesced to the subjectivistic interpretation of the religious act. Such an approach sees in man's relationship to his Creator only a subjective performance, exhausting itself in a peculiar state of mind, in a unique inner experience that, in turn, can never be translated into normative pressure and action. For the subjectivist, the meeting with God does not obligate man to anything, demands nothing of the finite being. It gives everything without asking for anything in return. Religion, according to the subjectivist, is not a regulative discipline, nor an exacting ethos, nor a doctrine of good and evil. It is an experience, an adventure, a drama; it reveals no law, it requires of man no specific mode of living.

The teaching of Judaism differs from subjectivist religion in several ways. Abraham was not only the first to proclaim the existence of God as Creator of the universe, but also the first to proclaim the presence of a moral law which can be traced back to God. The encounter of God with man expresses itself not only in a metaphysical-supernatural revelation of *kevod Elokim* (*majestas Dei*), but also in exposing man to *hesed Elokim* (*caritas Dei*), in which man may share, and which involves the supreme norm of *imitatio Dei*. Revelation is not only a great experience but also a legislative act. As such it is the revelation of the norm to Abraham: "For I knew him that he would command his house after him to keep the way of God" (Gen. 18:19). Who revealed to Abraham the way of God if not God Himself!

God is also the Creator of the world. His infinite will has legislated not only the moral law but the cosmic law as well. Since God is One, His will can be conceived of only in terms of an absolute unity. To maintain that the moral norm and the natural law stem from separable wills, one mechanistic and the other purposeful, would be tantamount to denying the unqualified oneness of God. If that separation is maintained, then the conclusion is obvious. There is either no moral norm, and teleological activity on the part of God is an absurdity, since the dynamics of the cosmos that He has instituted is mechanical; or the cosmic law itself is an expression of Divine grace and morality.

Judaism accepts the implications of this idea of God as Creator. The sentence in the Bible: "And God saw all that He had done and it was very good" (Gen. 1:21) indicates the moral character of creation, full of goodness and love. *Majestas Dei*, in other words, is manifest in the world, in its dynamics, complexity and orderliness. It is nothing but *caritas Dei*, the overflowing Divine grace, which permeates every nook and cranny of creation. The natural order is rigid, but it is only the shell into which grace has been encased, the utensil into which a steady stream of kindness continually pours. Natural law is the guise through which the moral law expresses itself. Its essence is good, in spite of the fact that quite frequently we experience the natural order as incurably unsympathetic and loveless. God's will wears a cosmic mask of harshness, automation and formality. The numen, in all of its appearances (both presence and absence), at all levels, hides the kerygma within its strange order: *Majestas Dei* is the garment covering *caritas Dei*.

Judaism, furthermore, maintains that the proper method of interpretation has been formulated in the Torah. The Torah is not to be understood as a sum total of quantitative knowledge or as a collection of dicta or pearls of wisdom, a code of laws and customs. It is far more than that. It is a method, a way, not only of doing things, but also of thinking things, of interpreting life, existence, world, man and, finally, God. The term Torah, with its etymological connotation of pointing, showing and guiding, emphasizes the methodological rather than the static and formulated. As such, the Torah's main objective is the translation of the numinous into the kerygmatic, the translation of the non-sensical and absurd into the vernacular of the teleological and rational. The Torah aims to discover *caritas* in *majestas*, kindness in beauty, familiarity in strangeness. Only through the Torah do we begin to understand the meaning of these orders.

Our previous discussion dealt with the loneliness of man at an individual-community level. However, man is also lonely at a cosmic plane. I would say that this feeling of loneliness is more grisly and tormenting than the previous experience in terms of the I-thou separateness. This form of solitude expresses a feeling of having fallen away from being, in transcendental uprootedness in spite of immanent rootedness. Man must be rooted, not only within himself, but also without himself. In his existential experience he must identify himself with origin, with cause, with ontic unity. He must feel one with the Father and Creator.

Can man achieve this? God Himself appears to us both as *Deus absconditus* and as *Deus revelatus*, as numen and kerygma. Man, however, can establish communion only with God

Who reveals Himself, not with God Who hides.

Prayer is the mirror of the lovesick religious soul. To understand how prayer enables man to establish communion with God requires us to analyze the religious-liturgical elements of our principal texts. The next four chapters will examine some of the texts pertaining to the *Shema*, the acceptance of the yoke of Heaven. We shall then return to an analysis of the text of the *Amidah*.

🦋 Intention (Kavvanah) in Reading Shema and in Prayer

Objective and Subjective Fulfillment of Mitzvot

As we discussed at the beginning of chapter two, the Halakhah distinguishes between two kinds of *mitzvot* (precepts): the objective and subjective. An objective halakhic precept denotes a duty whose fulfillment consists in a concrete physical performance. The Halakhah has a particular way of ordering all the functions of our life, whether they are technical, physiological, artistic, or anything else. It selects a certain function, in itself insensate and devoid of content, and raises it to the level of a religious act. The technical performance itself becomes endowed with halakhic-religious significance and implies fulfillment of the *mitzvah*, the realization of the transcendental norm.

In this instance, the subjective attitude of the agent is not a basic component part of the *mitzvah*. This is true even if we should accept the maxim *mitzvot tzerikhot kavvanah*, that each *mitzvah*-performance must be an intentional act, motivated by a sense of duty (*Berakhot* 13a). Though the intention is necessary, according to this view, it is not an intrinsic moment of the performance itself. The normative gestures of *tefillin, matzah, lulav*, for example, assert themselves not in a state of mind but in a technical behavior.

A subjective halakhic norm, in contradistinction to the objective, signifies *mitzvot* realized through an inner experience, in a state of mind, in a spiritual act, in a thought, a feeling, or a volition. Although the Halakhah, being very distrustful of human subjective life because of its vagueness, transience and volatility, has introduced, even in the realm of subjective norms, concrete media through which an inward religious experience manifests itself, the real essence of the subjective *mitzvah* is confined to the spiritual component.

Intention (Kavvanah) and Avodah She-ba-Lev for Shema

Recitation of *Shema* and *tefillah*, in all probability, belong to the group of subjective norms. Just as in other subjective *mitzvot*, so, too, with regard to *Shema* and *tefillah*, we must discriminate between two aspects: the formal, external aspect, constituting the mere technique of the norm-fulfillment; and the original aspect, which expresses their very essence. The physical deed of reciting a fixed Biblical or rabbinic text is only an external act that serves as a medium through which the norm finds its objectivation and concretion. The intrinsic *mitzvah*-performance lies within a different dimension, namely, that of the great, all-inclusive God-experience.

The reading of *Shema* was designated, by the Halakhah and Aggadah, as *kabbalat ol malkhut Shamayim*, taking upon oneself the yoke of the kingdom of Heaven, the acknowledgement and acceptance of the absolute, universal and eternal authority of God. As we have noted, the recitation of the silent prayer

(*Amidah*) is termed by the same Halakhah and Aggadah as *avo-dah she-ba-lev*, service of the heart; i.e. worshipping God. Worship as service, or as acceptance of a yoke, occurs not through cultic ceremonials and formal service, but via an inner paradoxical movement of the soul. This movement includes both a flight to God and a withdrawal from Him. The full realization of the commandments of *Shema* and *tefillah* thus manifests itself in the great heterogeneous religious experience.

As I noted above, the very content of *kavvanah* with reference to *Shema* and *tefillah* differs basically from the *kavvanah* associated with other *mitzvot*. The latter require only normative heedfulness or an imperativistic motivation, and an intention of acting in accord with the Divine will, which decreed the norm. Thus intention, in these commandments, does not constitute an integral part of the religious gesture. By contrast, the *kavvanah* in regard to *Shema* and *tefillah* forms the core of accomplishment, the central idea and the intrinsic content of the *mitzvah*. It is not a mere modality, expressing only the "how" of the *mitzvah*-fulfillment (as it does in other *mitzvot)*, but rather is identical with the very substance and essence of the commandment. It implies, instead of imperativistic intentionality, a full-fledged, all-embracing and all-penetrating experience of God.

Kavvanah, while reading *Shema* or praying, is not to be equated with ordinary intention. It is rather identical with meditation, spiritual surrender, or the turning and directing of the heart unto the Lord. For it is the heart, and not the lips, which is called upon to turn toward God in the morning and in the evening. Most halakhic authorities concur, as we have already noted, that the technical reading of the *Shema*, or saying of the prayers, is not enough. The inward turning to God is of utmost significance. Thus, the Halakhah teaches that if one fails to direct his heart unto the Lord while reading the *Shema*—his obligation remains unfulfilled.

The above thesis, that *kavvanah* with regard to *Shema* is not to be identified with *kavvanah* concerning other *mitzvot*, appears to us a truism. Yet it crystallized relatively late in the halakhic literature, as we can see by examining a crucial Talmudic discussion and its interpretation in the medieval classics. The Mishnah *Berakhot* 2:1 states: "He was reading the Torah and the time for *Shema* arrived: if he directed his heart to read, he fulfilled the obligation." The Talmud, in interpreting this Mishnah, states:

> This implies that *mitzvot* require intention (*kavvanah*). What is the meaning of directing his heart to read? He is reading! This refers to a case where he is uttering the sounds (*kore le-haggiah*). (*Berakhot* 13a)

What is the meaning of the answer *be-kore le-haggiah*? Rashi and Tosafot did not distinguish between the two classes of *kavvanah*. In explaining this passage, they appear to equate *Shema* with other *mitzvot*. Rashi identifies *kore le-haggiah* with automatic unconscious reading. The individual is engaged in examining the text and does not intend to recite. By force of habit, without being aware of it, he pronounces the words as he examines them. Here he has not fulfilled his duty because such a performance belongs to the category of *mit'assek*—it is an act performed automatically. Tosafot disagree with Rashi's exposition and explain that *kore le-haggiah* is ineffective because it is incorrect reading. Both Rashi and Tosafot did not think in terms of a twofold *kavvanah* theory, nor did they place *Shema* on the level of a subjective norm, whose fulfillment is associated with an inner experience. That is why they tried to explain the inadequacy of *kore le-haggiah* along the general outline of *mit'assek*, signifying an automatic, incomplete performance.

We come across the distinction between *Shema* and other *mitzvot*, for the first time, in the commentary of Rabbi Solomon ben Adret (Rashba) and in the annotations by the disciples of Rabbi Yonah to *Berakhot* 13b. Here we encounter a clear unequivocal interpretation of the singularity of the *Shema* performance which expresses itself in *kabbalat ol malkhut Shamayim*, complete and unqualified surrender to God. Rashba emphasizes that this kind of *kavvanah* signifies, not only turning towards God, but also turning away from all other finite and relative values and interests.

It is quite probable that Maimonides anticipated this view. Quoting the Mishnah, he rules: "He who read *Shema* and did not attend during the first verse, i.e. "Hear O Israel," did not fulfill his obligation. As for the other verses of *Shema*, if he did not attend, he fulfilled his obligation, even if he was reading the Torah routinely or checking these sections of text (*maggiah*)" (*Hilkhot Kri'at Shema* 2:1).

The implication is clear. If the inadequacy of *kore le-haggiah* were due to the element of automation or incorrectness of reading, it would extend to all the verses of *Shema*. Since *kore le-haggiah* is declared inadequate only with regard to the first verse, Maimonides apparently defined its inadequacy solely in terms of the lack of *kavvanah*. It would be wrong to maintain that the *kavvanah* associated with the first verse, according to Maimonides, is identical with the universal *kavvanah* concerning *mitzvot* (as Nahmanides interprets) since Maimonides holds that the recital of all three sections is required by a Pentateuchic norm. It would be absurd to limit *kavvanah*, in the ordinary sense of the term, to the first verse, since all sections are of equal normative status.

However, if we should assume that the specific *kavvanah* concerning *Shema* denotes accepting the yoke of Heaven, we would understand why it is limited to the first verse, since it is the first verse that contains this central motif. By concentrating while reciting this verse, one actually includes the whole of *Shema* in the mental act of faith. Yet, despite this inference, we lack a clear statement by Maimonides defining the essence and the need of *kavvanah* while reading *Shema*, a definition that would correspond to his formulation for *kavvanah* with respect to prayer. *Tosafot ha-Ra'ah* and also *Talmidei Rabbenu Yonah* operate with the idea introduced by Rashba. Nahmanides (see *Milhamot ha-Shem* to *Rosh ha-Shanah* 7a in Rif pagination) rejects the theory of Rashba, which we have identified with Maimonides's view as well. He maintains that *Shema* is identical with other *mitzvot* insofar as *kavvanah* is concerned. If, he writes, we accept the liberal viewpoint that the fulfillment of a commandment is not bound to a normative frame of mind and hence intentional concentration (*kavvanah*) is not necessary— then reading *Shema* does not constitute an exception to the rule and the technical recitation of the sections is sufficient. With the exception of Nahmanides, however, who rules out the special element of meditation required for *Shema*, most *Rishonim* since then, distinctly, and often intuitively, equate the norm of *kri'at Shema* with an experience of accepting the yoke of Heaven.

As a matter of fact, the Mishnah and the Baraita use the term *kabbalat ol malkhut Shamayim* to describe the recital of *Shema*. The addendum *Barukh shem kevod malkhuto* (Blessed be the glory of His kingdom) is indeed an interpretation of the first verse in terms of acceptance of and submission to the Kingdom of God.

From Halakhic Performance of Kavvanah to Religious Ideal

Maimonides discusses *avodah she-ba-lev* as expressing the ideal of perennial fellowship and friendship with God, in his *Guide* (3:51). It is important to note that Maimonides is not developing a halakhic thesis here. The Halakhah has its own standards and laws and cannot always align itself with mystical craving and longing. In addition, the Halakhah, as an exoteric discipline, must make its norm accessible and realizable to all, philosopher and simpleton, mystical and pragmatic mind alike. Of course, halakhic premises may serve, from time to time, as Archemedian fulcra, from which a God-intoxicated and lovesick soul makes the great leap from finitude into infinity.

Nonetheless, the Halakhah cannot and should not put up requirements such that only a select few are able to fulfill them. In the *Guide,* Maimonides asserts and formulates the purpose of religious action—complete involvement with the God-experience. He preaches a moral ideal of continuous fellowship with God. Not all halakhically adequate performances extend into the transforming experience of spiritual attachment. Hence, the Maimonidean doctrine of *avodah she-ba-lev,* taught in the *Guide,* where it refers to a perennial cleavage to God, is an esoteric one.

Yet, while discoursing on the devotional and mystical goal of all religious actions, a state of mind characteristic only of the great geniuses of religion, Maimonides introduces a halakhic motif which is of utmost importance to all of us. In expounding the way to attain Divine friendship and continual communion, he inserts a parenthetic remark of great relevance. He advises us to proceed gradually. The first mental exercise should consist in expanding the norm of spiritual concentration, or unqualified devotion and surrender, to religious areas where the Halakhah does not require such a meditative devotional attitude. Gradually one learns the practice of employing oneself entirely, with all one's faculties, in the service of God. By gradual and systematic training, one will finally learn to keep nothing from God and to make a full sacrifice. He writes as follows:

> The first thing you must do is this: Turn your thoughts away from everything while you read *Shema* or during the *tefillah,* and do not content yourself with being devout when you read the first verse of *Shema* or the first paragraph of the prayer. When you have successfully practiced this for many years, try, in reading the law or listening to it, to have all your heart and all your thought occupied with understanding what you read or hear (*Guide* 3:51, Friedlander translation, 387).

Thus, in the course of expounding his religious method, Maimonides lets it be known that *kavvanah* in reference to the first verse of *Shema* signifies the unique experience that we call accepting the yoke of Heaven. If he had concurred with Nahmanides in equating *kavvanah* relative to *Shema* with the imperative intentionality applicable to other *mitzvot*—that is to say with a technical and conventional performance, not with a representation of the inward craving of the soul—then he would be recommending in the *Guide* not only the continual application of such a devotional experience to all religious performances, but also a different kind of experience. In other words, the halakhic performance would be technical, while the experience recommended in the *Guide* would be subjective. That Maimonides failed to distinguish between the kind of intention required by the Halakhah and that demanded of the mystic proves our point: that Maimonides accepted the doctrine of subjectivism with regard to *Shema*. Moreover, he treats *Shema* and *tefillah* in an identical manner, implying that he identifies the subjective correlate of both *mitzvot*. Thus, Maimonides' view on *kavvanah* in *tefillah* applies to *Shema* as well. Maimonides himself qualifies and defines the essence of *kavvanah* relative to both: "to have all your heart and all your thought occupied with understanding what you read or hear." This comprises comprehension of the subject matter, which means, *eo ipso*, exclusive involvement in the performance.

Shema Contrasted with Tefillah (Prayer)

As stated before, we shall adopt this idea of subjectivism relative to *Shema* and *tefillah* though it is not unanimously asserted in the medieval classics. Our task will consist in analyzing and formulating the component parts of *kabbalat ol malkhut Shamayim*, on the one hand, and *avodah she-ba-lev*, on the other hand. The experience of God associated with *Shema* is called accepting the yoke of Heaven; the one connected with prayer is called service of the heart. Of course, there are elements of affinity and kinship between them. Nevertheless, each one represents a different awareness, a separate mode of expressing the experience of God. I might say that each one is typical of a specific "temperament," of a singular approach to God.

Let us formulate the basic difference between the interior experience of *Shema* and that of *tefillah*. Let us start with *tefillah*. *Avodah she-ba-lev* asserts itself in the great experience of Divine presence, the awareness of God, of His proximity and closeness to us. In service of the heart, the finite being encounters his infinite, invisible God, stands before Him and addresses himself to Him. The praying soul is sensitive to the unseen Presence, responsive to its word. *Tefillah* is considered a dialogue, a conversation, a colloquy between God and man, between Infinity and finitude, Being and nothingness. Man does not talk about God as a third person, as someone who is not there. He employs the thou, the grammatical form which brings together two unique individualities, which draws the inaccessible thou into the bounded I, and the mysterious I into the strange Thou. The thou in prayer drives finitude to its very boundary. What is more, it lets finitude transcend itself and join infinity. In short, in prayer man establishes contact with God—the miracle of revelation repeats itself.

Unlike *Shema*, prayer, as the awareness of Divine presence, is a more subjective, informal, private affair. It is so intimately, so inseparably and so inextricably interwoven with the whole of the human personality, that it remains an ineffable mystery. It eludes the power of the logos and ethos, which, many a time, venture to mold the inexpressible and indistinguishable into well-formulated and clearly distinct ideas and norms. Prayer is like a rising river during the spring thaw, refusing to follow the direction of the bounded riverbed, inundating its environs with elemental, primordial and uncontrollable force. The whole human personality becomes involved in that great transcendental universe; it is overwhelmed by its power, flooded by its light, and completely drawn into this marvelous state, in which man joins God. Hence, it would be a nonsensical undertaking on the part of philosophy to interfere with such total commitment, with the outright, unqualified giving of oneself to God, by trying to define it in terms of logical analysis. If prayer is total sacrifice, total surrender, then all attempts at classifying it under conventional headings are fallacious. The intellect, the will, the emotional life of the praying person, are occupied, enthralled and dominated by the encounter with God. The whole self stands before, converses with and feels Him. All faculties in the human mobilize their total energy to carry out the greatest of all functions—the revelation of man to God. All faculties enter into, grasp and appreciate this great experience of establishing oneself in the presence of God, of conversing face to face with Him (*kata theon*). Intrinsically, the state of prayer is a mystical experience not confined to a single area of our personality.

Reading *Shema* does not entail the state of consciousness required for prayer. "Accepting the yoke of Heaven" is not tantamount to entering the Divine presence. The state of reading *Shema* is not identical with that single mood in which man is driven into the company of God. For the performance of *Shema* is not the movement of going and coming to God. It is rather a sedate, placid experience. No encounter takes place. The element of the dialogue is lacking in this ritual. It expresses itself more in the form of declaration, confession, profession of faith. Whether this solemn profession takes the form of soliloquy, in which man declares and challenges himself, or a colloquy—in which he addresses himself to a thou—is irrelevant. What is important is the fact that if there is a thou in *Shema*, the thou is not God but a finite being like myself.

Of course, God is also experienced when one reads *Shema*, but not in a sense of fellowship or communion via the grammatical thou. God, in the experience of reading *Shema*, is "He," the third person, the remote, transcendent Being Whose yoke we do accept, Whose will we must abide, Whose might we respect and fear, Whose authority we acknowledge, yet into Whose presence we must not venture, Whose Being is hidden from us. The emphasis in *Shema* is found in the phrase *malkhut Shamayim* (the kingdom of Heaven), the majesty of God, *majestas Dei*, whose main attribute is inaccessibility and remoteness on the one hand, and absolute might and power on the other.

Shema as Intellectual Commitment

The realization of accepting the yoke of Heaven consists in an intellectual as well as a volitional gesture. It asserts itself in an act of comprehension and asserts knowledge of God in the form of creed. Free assent to this creed comprises the inner essence of accepting the yoke of Heaven.

The term "knowledge," in this connection, should not be confused with formal, dogmatic, soulless and "cold" articles of theology or of metaphysical speculation, with abstract deductions devoid of life and warmth, or with assent as a hollow, meaningless acceptance. Neither is knowledge in our case just an opinion (however cogent and valid) nor is assent a mere nod of the head. One can hardly speak here of a technical operation, whether the state of mind is reached by thought or by formal acquiescence. Both knowledge and assent must be realized as an immediate awareness, a glowing and vivid experience, something real and dynamic, an ideal effort toward a Divinely organized and morally inspired existence, the adventure of a heroic life. Nevertheless, the quality of this experience is basically intellectual and logical, and it takes place within an imperativistic frame of mind. The very act of accepting the yoke of Heaven manifests itself in lifting intuition to the level of discursive thinking, converting the implicit into the explicit, that is to say, the objectivation of an inner experience via the medium of the religious logos.

Even the attitude of the reader of *Shema* implies full commitment and submission. The verse "with all your heart..." challenges us to total involvement. Yet, since the experience of companionship and intercourse is not required in the state of mind of the reciter, the claim to totality is actually realized in an intellectual act of knowing and assenting, not in feeling. The mind commits the whole self, though the latter has not yet responded. The self lets itself be consecrated, dedicated and pledged.

There is, however, an immeasurable difference between the experience of being consecrated by another part of the self, so to speak, as occurs in reciting the *Shema*, and the experience of self-consecration. Even when the consecration is accomplished via the intellect and the will, there is only a promise of dedication and commitment to something, which will only be fully realized in a latter phase. In one word, there is, at this point, consecration, yet not sacrifice. The miraculous act of offering oneself to God is realizable only in His presence, an experience that is absent from the *Shema* performance.

If I may draw on the Bible for a parable, I would say that in prayer we find ourselves placed like Isaac upon the altar with Abraham's knife suspended over us. In reading *Shema*, by contrast, we are still on Isaac's long journey from Beersheba to Mount Moriah, pledged and consecrated to God.

Divine Majesty in Prayer and Shema

In contrast with the theme of *Shema*, the theme of *tefillah* is not *majestas Dei* with its attendant motifs of remoteness and inaccessibility, but that of friendship and sympathy. Moreover the feeling of friendship in prayer should be experienced not only in terms of nearness and immediate presence but as an intimacy which prompts us to confide in God and reveal ourselves to Him, by addressing Him in the second person, by approaching Him as Thou, not as He. One may find himself in the company of a great person, whom he does not dare to encounter face to face and employ the grammatical thou. That is not the case with prayer. Prayer forms a conversation that joins two into one community.

Speech is not always a colloquy, a conversation that expresses a sympathetic community and a friendship. Many a time we address ourselves to others in the form of a monologue, which the "other" happens to overhear. The addressee never enters our presence as the second person thou does. He remains outside of ourselves as a third party, alien and remote. The crux of prayer manifests itself in a feeling of companionship with Him and mainly in experiencing Him face to face (*panim el panim*); in having my whole self talk not only towards Him but also *with* Him, confronting Him. The preposition "with" makes all the difference. Hence, the moment of *majestas* which spells strangeness, inapproachability, exclusiveness, and the He "capitalized" is superseded by the motif of the parent who is not only close, but also involved with the fate and destiny of his child. The King is always addressed in the third person; the Father, in the second.

Therefore, the mood in which *Shema* is recited is an intense response to the display of Divine might and power. It contrasts with that of the man engaged in prayer who is receptive to the grace of God. In *Shema* one assents to and accepts authority. In the *Amidah* one gives Himself to God Who, in His infinite grace, meets him on almost equal terms within a community created by the worship.

Halakhic Confirmation

Let us now take a look at the *halakhot* pertaining to *Shema* and *tefillah* (prayer), as codified by Maimonides, to see whether this analysis is valid. Since both *Shema* and *tefillah* require *kavvanah,* we might assume that the laws regarding *kavvanah* are identical in both cases. Yet, even a superficial glance suffices to convince us that the reverse is true. The Halakhah has sharply discriminated between *Shema* and prayer. First Maimonides defines intention *(kavvanah)* with reference to prayer in the following words:

> The mind should be distracted from all other thoughts and the one who prays should feel that he is standing in Divine Presence *(Hilkhot Tefillah* 4:16).

This is a clear and unequivocal definition. *Avodah she-ba-lev* signifies the experience of an encounter with God. However, in reading the *Shema*, no such exacting demand is made. The awareness of Divine Presence is not required for the *Shema*. All that is required is a full comprehension of the eidetic content of the subject-matter. The performance is of a cognitive strain against a volitional backdrop: that is to say, it pertains to knowledge and assent.

This definition of *kavvanah* should, by itself, resolve all doubts as to the difference between the fundamental meaning of prayer and that of accepting the yoke of Heaven. In addition, a multitude of other rules confirm this theory about prayer and *Shema*. There are specific laws pertaining to *tefillah* that do not apply to *Shema*. Prayer, for instance, requires the standing position. One reciting the *Amidah* must turn his face towards Jerusalem and the Temple Mount. This halakhah was formulated by Solomon, in his famous prayer at the dedication of the *Mikdash* (I Kings 8). Maimonides considers the injunction to be of Pentateuchic origin. At the very outset of *Hilkhot Tefillah*, describing the prayer service which Jews engaged in before the "standardized" text was introduced by the Great Assembly, he notes that one prays facing the *Mikdash* (*nokhah ha-Mikdash*); Daniel also practiced this custom (Rambam, *Hilkhot Tefillah* 1:3; Daniel 6:11).

Tefillah also requires correct posture: *tikkun ha-guf* (preparation of the body). Maimonides describes it as follows: "When he stands at prayer he must set his hands on his heart, his right on his left and stand like a slave before his master in a state of fear and he should not place his hands on his hips" (*Hilkhot Tefillah* 5:4).

Likewise, one is required to be dressed appropriately for *tefillah*. Maimonides formulated the law in a very terse sentence: "He must fix his garb first and make himself distinguished and majestic" (5:5). Another law insists upon *tikkun hamakom*, the adequacy of the place of worship. One should not stand on an elevation with his face turned to the wall. A laborer who is engaged in work on the top of a wall should descend to the ground (5:6-8). Furthermore, the Halakhah enjoins one to modulate his voice properly while reciting the prayers, and to perform the required genuflection, *keri'ah*, at the first and the penultimate *berakhot* (5:9-10).

All these laws are confined to *tefillah*. They do not apply to *Shema*. In regard to the latter, the Halakhah has ruled that one may read *Shema* in an ordinary posture, standing, walking, lying down or riding on an animal. Even if one is standing on the top of a tree or on a wall he reads the *Shema* in that place. (Maimonides, *Hilkhot Keri'at Shema* 2:2-4). Modulation of the voice, selection of a proper place, and other gestures which are needed for *tefillah* are completely irrelevant with reference to *Shema*. In addition, there are also some rules whose violation invalidates the performance of the *tefillah*: for instance, drunkenness or disturbing elements (*Hilkhot Tefillah* 4:17f). Again, these factors do not render the reading of *Shema* invalid. The term *tefillato to'evah* (the prayer is an abomination), which is used in connection with such situations, is inapplicable to *Shema*.

Let us look at another halakhic rule which further demonstrates the unique character of *tefillah*. As to *Shema* the Halakhah permits intermissions during the recital. If, while reciting *Shema*, one met other people or was accosted by them, he may interrupt his reading in order to salute them or return their greetings, in accordance with the particular rules formulated by the law with regard to such a situation. However, if such a meeting occurred during the recital of the *Amidah*, he must not interrupt in any case, regardless of the etiquette or the effect in terms of public relations. Even if the king approached him, he is enjoined from saluting or returning his greetings. (See *Mishnah Berakhot* 2:1-2 and *Hilkhot Keri'at Shema* 2:15-17, regarding interruption during *Shema*; regarding the *Amidah*, *Mishnah Berakhot* 5:1 and *Hilkhot Tefillah* 6:9.)

The unique character of *tefillah* is seen in other halakhic rulings as well. Concerning *Shema*, Maimonides accepted the view held by R. Yohanan that interrupted reading (*le-serugin*) is valid (*Rosh ha-Shanah* 34b; *Hilkhot Keri'at Shema* 2:12). In other words, one who pauses during the recital of *Shema* has fulfilled his duty, even if he paused between the reading of one verse and the next for an interval long enough to conclude the whole text. However, as regards *tefillah*, the ruling is different. There Maimonides took a stricter view and considered an intermittent recital of the *Amidah* insufficient. The individual who had to pause for a short time may, when the emergency passes, resume his prayers at the place where he interrupted the reading; but if the interval is sufficiently lengthy to have concluded the *Amidah* in that time, he must start from the beginning (*Hilkhot Tefillah* 4:13). Maimonides here discriminates between reading *Shema* and *tefillah*. The Alfassi before him, and Nahmanides after him, concurred with this opinion. The reason for this distinction was explained by Ravad and Nahmanides. They maintain that prayer, by its very nature, cannot be subject to interruption (*Megillah* 17b; Ravad's notes on Alfassi and Nahmanides, *Milhamot Ha-Shem* to *Berakhot* ch. 3 (15b-16a in Rif pagination)).

The Halakhah thus depicts *tefillah*, unlike *Shema*, as a singular performance that rules out all distractions and intermissions. At the same time, the Halakhah challenges man to adopt a very solemn and yet a humble mood, to understand that it is a difficult and extremely serious business, requiring attention, discipline, concentration, alertness, tension, humility, and awe. The complete surrender of oneself to God in the act of petition, supplication or in the singing of a hymn—these are the central motifs of *avodah she-ba-lev*. They entail the consciousness of Divine presence, the total commitment to an unconditional and unqualified association with God.

It is for this reason that all the liberal rules with regard to the recitation of *Shema* are invalid if applied to *tefillah*. *Shema* remains bounded by the intellectual-volitional sphere. *Tefillah*, by contrast, is an experience that claims everything in man and cannot take notice of social etiquette, communal obligations, political power, economic needs, or similar considerations. Prayers should not be recited at random, casually. Praying is a great, all-embracing passionate performance. Whatever is out-side the universe of prayer sinks into nothingness. The cosmos shrinks to just one point—at which God meets man. Everything else is submerged, dismissed, and forgotten.

On the Method of Investigation and the Role of the Berakhot

As we prepare to continue our investigation of the prayer-book, a new question, one pertaining to method, comes to the fore. If we are to give our attention to the experience associated with the reading of *Shema* and if we are to analyze the mean-ing, content and motifs of *Shema*, what method of research must be employed? By what criteria should we be guided in elaborating and developing our theme? For it is easy to suggest ideas, sometimes very ingenious; yet it is very hard to find objective standards by which we can measure and appraise the cogency and veracity of hypothetical explanation.

As to the appropriate method of research: It seems to me that there is a threefold approach to the analysis of the *Shema* experience: First and foremost, the Halakhah, with which we have already begun. I have always maintained that the halakhic elements constitute the most appropriate and reliable material out of which a philosophical understanding might emerge. If this approach is cogent in regard to other themes, it is certainly true of the recitation of *Shema,* which is, as has been maintained before, a subjective norm. The Halakhah has never left this motif out of sight. Therefore, the halakhic rules are very revealing as to the inner essence of the experience. Because the subjective elements are salient, the objectification process here has not gone through a multitude of phases and the objective element is closely correlated to the subjective correlate.

Second, there is the aggadic material: Here I must, of course, emphasize the need for great caution in order not to fall prey to one's own imagination and read into the texts alien ideas. Particularly those of us who are rabbis are prone to the homiletical approach. The tendency is to utilize the Aggadah as merely a point of departure or as a decorative motif, without full commitment to the cogency of our interpretation. We therefore must be especially careful not to substitute our own thought for that of the Aggadah. However, the undertaking is not a hopeless one, as long as we allow ourselves to remain on our guard and not drift on the tide of our own fantasy. From time to time it is good to check aggadic interpretations against halakhic ideas in order to ascertain the adequacy of our approach.

Lastly, in dealing with the texts we recite, we must consider the liturgy itself: I refer to the liturgical background of the texts. In the case of *Shema,* the Halakhah provided the recitation with an appropriate liturgical introduction and conclusion. *Shema* forms the central theme of something more lengthy and elaborate that serves as the framework of this great performance. In the evening and in the morning, *Shema* is preceded by two blessings. In the morning it is followed by one blessing, and by two in the evening. These blessings of the prologue and the epilogue to *Shema* are not to be identified with the conventional *birkot ha-mitzvah,* blessings that accompany a *mitzvah-*

performance. Rather, they constitute what I would term a commentary to the *Shema* reading. Each motif of *Shema* is isolated from the complex experience, elucidated and expressed in the form of hymn or entreaty. Thus, through the accompanying liturgy, the Halakhah actually continues to spin the yarn of *ker-i'at Shema*.

The Halakhah did not add anything new in the *berakhot*, anything that the original text of *Shema* did not contain. Rather, it takes an implicit motif and unfolds its meaning and sense. What is merely implied in *Shema* is explicated and interpreted by the *berakhot*. Hence, *Shema* and the *berakhot* form one whole, an integral entity in which the experience of accepting the yoke of Heaven asserts itself. The prologue and the epilogue are, so to say, footnotes and comments to *Shema* phrased in liturgical language. Since the basic quality of the commandment to recite *Shema* is realized through a definitive state of mind, with the performance being relegated to the level of *ma'aseh ha-mitzvah* (the external action), the Rabbis felt that one should not only recite the *Shema* but also engage in analyzing its motifs, stating distinctly its ideas and weaving out of them a liturgical texture which leads to the much greater engagement of *avodah she-ba-lev,* the *Amidah.*

The *berakhot*, therefore, are the liturgical equivalent of the Pentateuchic creed that is expressed in the three sections of the *Shema.* As a matter of fact, when we examine carefully the content of the *berakhot* we discover that each one corresponds to one section of the *Shema.* The first (*Yotzer Or* in the morning; *ha-Ma'ariv Aravim* at night), incorporates the motif of the first section of *Shema*: unity and Kingdom of God. The angels are depicted as accepting the yoke of Heaven.

The second *berakhah (Ahavah Rabbah* or *Ahavat Olam)* takes up the idea of revelation and the giving of the Law and so develops the main theme of the second section, *kabbalat ol mitzvot*, the acceptance of Divine authority and commitment to the realization of the religious norm. And finally the third

(*Ge'ulah*) which follows *Shema*, either in the formula of *emet ve-yatziv* (morning) or *emet ve-emunah* (evening), constitutes the liturgical correlate of the third section (*va-Yomer*), whose motto is the Exodus from Egypt, redemption. The fourth *berakhah*, *Hashkivenu*, recited only in the evening, is a continuation of the third *berakhah*, as it is described in the Talmud (*Berakhot* 4b) as a prolonged *ge'ulah*. Since the explication of the creed of *Shema* is the main objective of *birkot Shema*, they may serve as the most reliable and informative source as regards the basic elements of this creed.

With these remarks, I have completed my review of the basic differences between *Shema* and prayer and have also outlined the sources and material upon which a precise analysis of *Shema* will have to draw. Now I shall begin with the analysis itself and try to isolate the various elements involved in the comprehensive cognitive act of reading the *Shema*.

❧ The Essence of Shema: Unity of God, Love of God, and the Study of His Law

Maimonides, in defining the essence of *kabbalat ol malkhut Shamayim*, pointed to the three first verses of *Shema,* which contain three principles: 1) God is one; 2) love of God; 3) "that these words that I command you shall be upon your heart"—the study of Torah (*Hilkhot Keri'at Shema* 1:2). What prompted him to include in the great act of accepting the yoke of Heaven only these three verses to the exclusion of the *mitzvot* formulated in the following verses. In this, he is prompted by the opinion of the Tanna R. Eliezer who requires *kavvanah* in the recitation of these verses, "up to this point" (*Berakhot* 13a).

Rashi and the Tosafot school disagreed as to the exact extent of R. Eliezer's phrase "up to this point" in the passage just cited. Rashi included the first three verses; the Tosafists confine *kavvanah* to the first two verses ("Hear" and "You shall love") and exclude the third one, referring to Torah study, from this requirement (Rashi and Tosafot, *Berakhot* 13a s.v. *ad kan*). Maimonides apparently concurs with Rashi that *Shema* requires intention for the three verses, thus including the verse that alludes to the study of Torah. Since Rashi singled out these verses of *Shema*, it appears that they contain the basic components of *kabbalat ol malkhut Shamayim*. In his opinion, R. Eliezer included the commandment to study Torah. Tosafot inferred the same with regard to the two verses—namely God's unity and the commandments to love Him and study His Torah.

Prima facie it is perplexing to us that Maimonides should deduce the essence of the *Shema* from the halakhic premise of R. Eliezer, since his view was rejected by both R. Akiva and R. Meir and is not accepted by us as the standard halakhic ruling. On the one hand, R. Akiva thinks that one must exercise *kavvanah* while reading the entire first section, and, on the other hand, R. Meir advanced the opinion—which was sanctioned by the Halakhah—that only the reading of the first verse requires *kavvanah* (intention). Apparently, neither R. Akiva nor R. Meir held the view of R. Eliezer: that the first two or three verses contain all the themes that require intention.

The answer to this perplexing question is a simple one. Maimonides, upon examining the entire first section, arrived at the conclusion that R. Eliezer's opinion prevails with respect to the full halakhic definition of the components of accepting the yoke of Heaven. The last two verses, dealing with the commandments of *tefillin* and *mezuzah*, do not contain any new universal aspects to be integrated with the experience of accepting the yoke of Heaven. Neither constitutes a subjective norm which would introduce a new motif into the experience of *Shema*. As such, the last two verses belong instead to a different category—accepting the yoke of *mitzvot*, which forms the theme of the second section of *Shema*. There is no reason to prefer *tefillin* and *mezuzah* to other commandments with respect to their significance and meaning. Since these two areas are treated on a par with other norms, they are not part of the complex experience of accepting the yoke of Heaven. By contrast, Maimonides thought that the first three verses do entail something very important and significant, closely related to accepting the yoke of Heaven. *Kabbalat ol malkhut Shamayim* is not exhausted by an abstract cognitive act regarding the principle of unity, but includes also the element of free assent and consecration, exerting a power over the soul and a fascination which no other idea is able to raise.

This pledging of oneself, this self-consecration, is inextricably intertwined with the realization of the idea of love of God. The first verse ("Hear O Israel") presents a cognitive premise, which lays the foundation and provides us with the intellectual motif for the second performance—assent and commitment. Hence, Maimonides maintained that there is unanimity of opinion, among the Talmudic sages, as to the content of accepting the yoke of Heaven. It is experienced in a threefold theme: unity of God, love of God, study of His Torah.

The question about the qualitative content and structure of the *kavvanah* is not identical to the whole controversy between R. Eliezer and the other sages about the extent of the required *kavvanah*. That dispute among the *Tanna'im* concerns only a quantitative aspect: they debated which part of *Shema* must be read in such a state of mind. Is it incumbent upon the reader to concentrate during the recital of the whole section, or does one significant part of it, read attentively with full awareness of the basic motif, suffice? On this point, the *Tanna'im* disagreed; R. Akiva believed that this awareness should last throughout the first section while R. Meir confined it to the first verse, and R. Eliezer took an intermediary position. However, as to the meaning and essence of accepting the yoke of Heaven, all concurred that the first three verses cover the whole area of that experience. Neither does R. Akiva insist upon injecting the norms of *tefillin* and *mezuzah* into the great experience, nor does R. Meir suggest that *Shema* can be stripped of the great resolve and free assent expressed in the commandment to love God.

Unity of God and the Chain of Tradition

Our task is now to interpret and expound these three basic motifs that comprise accepting the yoke of Heaven. The first motif is the unity of God, formulated in the first verse of the *Shema*.

Before we begin to delve into metaphysical intricacies, it is appropriate to examine an aggadic passage which has been passed on to us in different sources. The mere fact that the story occurs in so many aggadic treatises concerned with *Shema* attests to its central significance and universal symbolism. Even Maimonides, who very seldom cites aggadic sources, relates this beautiful story (see *Hilkhot Keri'at Shema* 1:4). Let us investigate its philosophical meaning. The Talmud, explaining the presence of the hymnal refrain *Barukh shem kevod malkhuto* (Blessed is the Name of the Glory of His kingdom) after the first verse of *Shema*, draws on a tradition according to which the practice of reciting the *Shema* in that way, inserting the refrain, goes back to Jacob and his sons at their last encounter:

> Jacob wished to reveal to his sons the end of days, but the Holy Spirit withdrew from him. He said: "Perhaps, Heaven forbid, there is a defect in my bed, like Abraham from whom Ishmael was engendered, and my father Isaac, from whom Esau was engendered." His sons said to him: "Hear O Israel, the Lord is God, the Lord is one. Just as there is only One in your heart, so there is only One in our hearts." Then did our father Jacob recite, "Blessed is the Name of the Glory of His kingdom forever" (*Pesahim* 56a. For parallels, see, for example, *Bereshit Rabbah* 98:4; *Sifre* to Deut. 6:4; *Devarim Rabbah* 2:25).

Despite some variations among the sources, the gist of the story is identical in all versions. In some the words *bikkesh le-gallot et ha-ketz* (he wished to reveal the end of days) are missing, and the phrase "perhaps there is a defect in my bed" is replaced by "perhaps you harbor in your hearts dispute against He who spoke and the world was," to which challenge the sons reply, "Just as there is no dispute in your heart so there is none in ours." Maimonides drew on the *Sifre* and midrashic sources along with the talmudic passage. He left out Jacob's failure to foresee the end and instead interpolated into his inquiry the words "one who is not with us respecting the unity of God," the equivalent of the midrashic doubt about God's unity. Maimonides also expounded the words *Shema Yisrael* as "Hear Israel, our father," the sons addressing themselves to Jacob. All this confirms that Maimonides was exploiting the midrashic texts. At the same time, however, he employed the expression "perhaps there is a defect in you" which was used by the talmudic source. This establishes that he availed himself of a composite version.

What message does this narrative convey to us? First, that the creed of *Shema* goes back to the very origin of our history, to the dawn of our collective existence. The solemn declaration is perhaps the first truth, which our great Patriarchs discovered. It became their motto and dominant motif in life. It is not merely a theoretical truth, a philosophical pronouncement, a religious dogma, a norm, however central and endowed with meaning. It is rather the shibboleth of our historical uniqueness, a living doctrine which bears witness to our charismatic quality and which keeps us together as one, spanning almost the whole course of ages, uniting us with our Patriarchs, drawing them into our temporal ontic circle, thus lending to our own existence the tenor of "timelessness." The midrashic version stresses the paradoxical idea that the reading of *Shema* is a solemn and vigorous response to Jacob's challenge of old, which rings through the distances of time. It is indeed the acceptance of a great task, the declaration addressed to the remote past that joins the march of generations committed to one idea. In a word, the reading of *Shema* is a dialogue between the ages, the continual restaging of the historic meeting of Jacob and his sons, pregnant with paradoxical destiny, full of import.

In prayer, we experience the presence of God; we stand near and commune with Him. In reading the *Shema,* by contrast, we enter the presence of those persons who walked with Him, we stand in their shadow; we converse with men who, though they died a biological death, have been reincarnated time and again in our historical experience via divergent media and various forms of existence. The great drama of destiny, begun by the Patriarchs, is reenacted again. Searching for and finding God, struggling with fate, absorbing defeat and yet emerging victorious—all these mark continuity of Being amid a changing world. This experience is explicated through this reading of *Shema.* God is one and this spells oneness of historical event.

The first principle—accepting the yoke of Heaven—on this reading, asserts itself in this analysis, in an act of self-identification with the historical destiny of our people, in the experience of oneness of ages and events, the merger of the multidimensional time-feeling into one focal point, a point that is, *eo ipso,* the center of my own self. It asserts itself in the pouring of the individual stream of existence into the mighty sea swept by the hurricane of historic occurrence, enveloped in the mists of past and future, meeting with the thought, longing and will of a world physically long gone yet metaphysically still living, great and awesome.

There is, however, a second aspect to the creed proclaimed in *Shema.* The theme of *Shema* has not only been communicated to us through an apocalyptic revelation as a truth that is metalogical and transcendental. It was also discovered and ascertained by the human mind itself, employing its natural categorial instruments of apprehension and comprehension. Revelation only confirmed what the logos had already attained. Jacob is the representative of a natural ethical system of the charismatic community who went forth to find God and discover His ways, relying on his own wits and talents. Moses, who was found by God and taken prisoner by Him in the great encounter of revelation, proclaimed the same truth—*Shema Yisrael*. The logos is capable of arriving at an apocalyptic truth. Hence, the experience connected with *Shema* is not something mysterious and paradoxical, which man can only accept but not comprehend. It is an august truth rooted in the logos and reaching out to the deepest strata of the human personality. It begins with the awakening of the logical awareness of man, with the ripening of his thoughts and insights, with the dawning upon him of the greatest of all questions—the question of origin and root. That occurs with the advent of the Patriarchs. Hence, the experience is consummated at the level of naturalness and rationality, when man begins to examine himself and his surroundings.

Analyzing Divine Unity

Having expounded the double motif in the aggadic narrative, namely the historical oneness and logico-cognitive discovery of the Divine unity and government of the world, we must presently consider the idea of unity in all its aspects.

In undertaking this analysis, we shall employ the halakhic-midrashic method instead of the scholastic. The latter has always started with abstract theological propositions and postulates, proceeding gradually from the abstract and general to the concrete and particular. (Some great theologians modeled their systems after Euclidean geometry—*more geometrico*—and therefore their method was always the deductive one.) Hence, theological wisdom has always preceded the ethical and practical disciplines. If the mode of shaping propositions of a religious nature must employ the deductive method, then the scholastic procedure is correct. Judaism acknowledges the cogency of such a process of thinking: the Decalogue is based upon deduction—the first commandment serves as the general premise from which all laws are inferred.

Yet, Judaism also devised the inductive approach. Here one begins, not with the fundamental and general, but with the particular, with ethico-religious realities, new and raw facts; applying the method of generalization and abstraction, one arrives at universal principles. The Halakhah has, with a few exceptions, always availed itself of the latter method. We seldom encounter abstract rules and axioms in the Mishnah and Talmud. This literature operates with particular cases, episodes, and specific problems. In this multitude of details and particular points one is supposed to look for definitive patterns and general rules which assert themselves in this divergent material. Halakhic creativity is based on nothing but the power of exploring the manifold to uncover the uniform, of searching the seemingly disparate and unconnected to find the kindred, of studying the concrete and immediate to formulate the abstract and remote.

The principle of the unity of God is the very foundation of our faith, whose witnesses and defenders we all are, even to the end of time. Is it also a halakhic postulate, from which definitive conclusions or practical values follow, a principle on which our laws and government are molded, our politics and ethics founded, or is it only an article of faith which, though professed by us, embodying the very essence of our philosophy, though laying hold of our very lives, is not translated into halakhic laws and rules of conduct, and does not found a practical equation? If the latter be true then an application of the inductive approach would be ruled out from the outset. If, however, the first assumption is correct, our task would be to find the halakhic revelations of this great truth.

Since the inductive method has been so successfully employed by the Halakhah, we shall employ it in our present analysis of the reading of *Shema*. Indeed, this sustained orientation is a sublime principle of halakhic thinking. Accordingly, we shall not delve at once into the philosophical-metaphysical and theological aspects of the principle of unity of God. Instead, we shall give our attention to more practical facets of this idea, as it is manifested on all levels of community and individual attention. Let us explore first the peripheral expansion of this truth. Only then shall we proceed toward the center, from the conclusion to the premise.

Divine Unity and Its Practical Implications

Maimonides defined the commandment of unity twice, once in *Mishneh Torah*, and once in *Sefer ha-Mitzvot*. Let us examine his formulations: we might find there some clue to our problem. In *Mishneh Torah*, he writes:

> God is one. He is not two, nor more than two, but one. His uniqueness is unlike that of other unities existing in the universe. He is not one like a species, which contains many unities, nor like a body that is divided and bounded... Knowing this truth is a positive commandment as it is written: The Eternal, our God, is one God *(Hilkhot Yesodei ha-Torah* 1:7).

In this passage, Maimonides defined the precept of unity only in cognitive, intellectual terms. The norm enjoins us not only to believe but also to comprehend and interpret this article of faith, as far as the human mind is capable, in logico-noetic categories. He does not mention the practical significance of this principle concerning human conduct.

In *Sefer ha-Mitzvot,* however, the tenor of the formula is suggestive of a halakhic-practical motif:

> We are commanded in the belief of His unity, that we are to believe that the Agent of existence and its First Cause is one. And this is Scripture's statement, "Hear O Israel..." In many rabbinic texts you will find them saying "in order to make My Name one,"... This means that He indeed took us out of bondage and performed the acts

of kindness and benefit that He did on condition that we believe in His unity as we are obligated to. They also call this commandment "the kingdom of Heaven" for they say "in order to accept the kingdom of Heaven," meaning the confession of His unity and belief in it (Positive Commandment 2).

The differences between the passage in the *Code* and the one here are easily discernible. First, in the Hebrew translation of *Sefer ha-Mitzvot* Maimonides speaks of *emunah* (faith), instead of knowledge. The term *yedi'ah* (knowledge) does not appear in the Hebrew *Sefer ha-Mitzvot* text. The emphasis is laid upon *emunah*-belief. Second, the principle of unity, in the *Sefer ha-Mitzvot*, is connected to the original covenant between God and Israel, from which the people of Israel derives charismatic endowment and which constitutes the legal basis for the continuation of the community relationship. In other words, the singular historical occurrence of the Jewish people finds both its root and apex, its uniqueness and legitimation, in our faith in the unity of God. While in *Mishneh Torah* the whole doctrine has been placed on the level of metaphysics or theology, the *Sefer ha-Mitzvot* alters the dominant theme from the metaphysical or theological to the historical.

Since Maimonides promoted the idea of unity to the rank of a history-shaping, destiny-determining principle, it cannot be confined to the abstract metaphysical realm. The doctrine of unity, as a stipulation in the covenantal charismatic relationship must be provided with practical and halakhic-ethical moments, subject to historical activation. Otherwise it would forfeit all of its validity. It would be fallacious for Maimonides to maintain that the conditional character of the covenant depends solely upon a hollow act of professing some dogma, upon formal acceptance. The covenant is rather a law to be practiced and realized in the world of fact and deed. In short, the unity of God is not only the foundation of our noetic experience but also the source of our ethical-moralistic awareness. Besides being a noetic idea, it is a halakhic, ethical norm that expresses itself in a variety of practical ways.

This inference is consonant with the general theory that I have developed: that Judaism activates all its abstract ideas and articles of faith in the halakhic-ethical sphere. They are charged with dynamic-imperativistic qualities, which mark out their practical course and cast them into the form of norms. Divine unity, as the foremost principle within our system, is certainly replete with an enormous ethico-halachic momentum that expresses itself through the basic ethical tendencies of our people. The question remains: what are the ethico-halachic laws whose root and origin is the principle of unity? What are the manifestations of this great truth, which has kindled the imaginations of countless generations and brought fire to their hearts?

The most pervasive practical expression of this eternal truth is to be found in the great and yet grim determination of our people to defend its beliefs and laws even to torture and death. The martyrdom of the Jewish saints, unequalled and unrivaled in the annals of human history, is the most impressive and awesome manifestation of the doctrine of unity as a halakhic-ethical principle to which one is committed and consecrated. Let us scrutinize this practical expression. The Talmudic narrative of the martyrdom of R. Akiva associates the spirit of self-sacrifice, which this great saint evinced with such courage and superhuman heroism, with the indomitable faith in unity of God. This principle accounts for the historical phenomenon of Jewish martyrdom.

> When they took R. Akiva out to be killed it was the time for reading *Shema*, and they were flaying his flesh with iron combs, while he was accepting the yoke of the kingdom of Heaven. His disciples said to him: "Our master, to this extent?" He said to them: "All my life I was sorry

about this verse—'with all your soul,' even if He takes your soul. I said, when will I be able to fulfill it. Now that it has come to me, shall I not fulfill it?" He prolonged the word *Ehad* until he expired. A voice spoke: "Happy are you R. Akiva, that your soul expired at *Ehad*" (*Berakhot* 61b).

The precept of *kiddush Ha-Shem* (sanctification of the divine Name) is rooted in the ideology evolved by the reading of *Shema*. The message conveyed in the single word *Ehad* (One) challenges us to incur death and suffering, if by doing so we defend this great truth of ours. In the Talmudic discourse on the commandment of *kiddush Ha-Shem*, the Halakhah infers from the phrase *be-khol nafeshekha* ("with all your soul") that one is duty-bound in certain situations to surrender his life rather than to transgress the Law (Mishnah *Berakhot* 9:5 and *Hilkhot Yesodei ha-Torah* 5:7).

What corroborates the aggadic tradition connecting R. Akiva's martyrdom with the concept of the unity of God? Although the Halakhah deduces the precept of *kiddush Ha-Shem* from the phrase "with all your soul," it is apparent that the cognitive origin is the idea implied in *Ehad*. We have emphasized that the second verse signifies an act of consecration and self-dedication, while the first verse conveys to us a truth, a noetic message, which finds its realization on a dynamic-ecstatic level of love. Maimonides, in *Sefer ha-Mitzvot*, discussing the precept of *kiddush Ha-Shem*, writes:

> [W]e are commanded to make public this true belief in the world and are not to fear any harm, even when compulsion is brought to bear to coerce us we shall not attend to its agent but surrender ourselves to die, and shall not mislead him to think that we had denied even while believing in God in our hearts... And in the language of *Sifra*: "On this condition did I take you out of

Egypt, that you sanctify My Name in public (Positive Commandment 9).

By professing and committing ourselves to the faith in Divine unity we have *eo ipso* pledged our lives in the defense of this truth. Maimonides even refers to the same clause in the covenant relationship, which he mentions with regard to the precept of unity itself. The Jewish community, in establishing its unique fellowship with God, has consecrated itself to uphold this fellowship even at the cost of its own life.

In view of this practical manifestation of the doctrine of unity of God we may say that the idea of Divine unity, besides being a theoretical truth, also expresses an axiological "truth." In proclaiming "the Lord our God, the Lord is one," we express a value judgment, make known an act of appraising and measuring the objective worth of our ideals. We deal here not only with a cognitive situation, a metaphysico-noetic idea, but also with a valuing situation.

Judaism placed the emphasis upon an axiological tenor rather than upon the solely noetic aspect. The Greek mind was engaged in a perennial quest for the true. The mysterious relationship between truth and reality fascinated the greatest minds. By truth they understood the equivalent of the *to ontos*, the real being, that which is identical with itself, persistent and lawful. They discriminated between true being and half-being, or non-being. The former signifies ontic patterns, which come within the purview of the logos. In other words, they were interested in such aspects of existence that express a continuum of interdependence, either on a noetic or dynamic level; the eidetic or causal continuum. In accordance with this approach, knowledge means inferring, deducing, understanding the simple phenomenon in the light of the general.

The Greeks, however, had no understanding for the realm of values, for what is axiological, for what is valid, for the ideal (not the real). The imperative, the norm as such, did not impress them. All Greek ethical systems are eudaemonistic, concerned with happiness and well-being as their goal. The ethic is only a techne, a means, a skill, a formula that leads to an end. Even Plato's philosophy, where the ethical motif is dominant, is not a deflection from this general line of thought. Judaism introduces the "ought;" it uncovered a new realm, which captivates the human mind, arousing its curiosity, motivating and guiding its unfolding and development. Judaism beheld not the idea of being as a function, but the idea of being as an action, as an ideal, as a telos, as a value; in short, the ethical being. While the Greek mind was exploring the being as a datum, Judaism was trying to grasp it as a task, a mission, an ideal to be verified and a value to be realized.

Truth, itself, is not only a noetic problem but also an ethical one. There is a truth norm implied in the theoretical awareness. The scientist knows that the attainment of truth is an imperative, not merely a useful performance. People fought for scientific truth even when their championship of it spurred martyrdom and certain death. Thus, there is a normative motif in the ontic awareness as such. "To be" is an ethical goal entailing commitment to something, not only a fact to be accepted, or a theoretical mystery to be unraveled. Being challenges us to pledge ourselves to its realization, instead of surrendering to its factual impact.

This is why the Jew has never encountered the great and perplexing problem of the tragic in life. If life is an actus, a performance through which an ideal is attained, then it is endowed with meaning, and wherever the meaningful prevails, the tragic, which, for the Greek mind, was associated with the absurd, turns into the grandiose, sublime and sacred. Life as a factum is tragic; as an action, life is great. Purposiveness and meaning are imparted to suffering.

While the Greeks, in their search for truth in life, employed the logos as their single instrument in attaining their objective, Judaism introduced a new mode of approach: appreciating, appraising, valuing and pledging ourselves to truth. A new situation developed in which one does not have to be a Socrates or a Plato in order to live a full life. There is another medium through which man can raise his existence to the higher ontic level—the normative halakhic method. Life is considered to be an ethical affair, basically exoteric and simple. The metaphysical dimension has been supplemented by the ethico-halakhic. Being is comprehended not in metaphysical-causal but in ethico-normative categories. As a matter of fact, however, the cognitive method, though very helpful in bettering physical conditions, cannot assist man in his search for the meaningful and for ontic worth. Knowing, on a relational-formal level, all the causal links in the chain of being, does not endow knowledge with that mysterious quality which makes existence a teleological, freely-willed and worthwhile affair. Since being, as such, is not specifically a changing situation, God is not only conceived, but also appreciated as the highest value.

The awareness we have described here is engendered by our idea of God's unity, and the practical devotion on our part to defend our belief to the point of death.

The idea of Divine unity comes to practical expression, not only in its extreme manifestation of martyrdom, but also in the way Judaism grasps the relation between the one God, Creator of the universe, and the world He has made. The next two chapters will bring us back, via an analysis of the first blessing which precedes the morning *Shema* (*Yotzer Or*), to the themes we have arrived at here.

Immanence and Transcendence: Comments on Birkat Yotzer Or

One Divine Will

Judaism is a theistic religion. The philosophy of theism it proclaimed to the world spells out more than Divine omnipotence and God's unlimited ability to intervene in the cosmic drama and to determine its course and unfolding in accordance with His will. It also implies that the universe is an unfinished and incomplete process; this being the case, the creative Divine act is continuous. Moreover, creation is tantamount to revelation, via the orderliness, lawfulness and precision of the creature. The world is not a mechanism organized by the artisan, which functions automatically, uses up its energy, and runs its course to complete disintegration, as the law of entropy implies, but is a living purposive creature, expressing the Divine will embedded in organic and inorganic nature. That Divine will manifests itself in the relational mathematical complexities of the universe as well as in its inner recesses. Being, both as an essence and as an occurrence, manifests an infinite will engaged in the great enterprise of creation.

To exist means to be created. Continuity of existence means perennial creation. Being, in a word, is not a factum but an actus, an emergence of God, an uninterrupted process of revelation. God reveals Himself within the cosmos, within the regularity and sequence. He speaks to man both through the abstract scientific cosmos, which is relational, formal and ideal, and through the immediate, living, avid concrete and fleeting world of sense perception and sensation. Being, in all its dimensions, is a revelation. God wills the cosmic process and speaks through it.

The Divine name *Elokim* signifies the immanence of God in creation, abiding within the particularity of the grains of sand on the sea-shore, in the bursting forth of the white blossoms in the spring, in the rise and fall of the sea, and in the nebulae flying off into endless distances. Every phenomenon is born out of a Divine actus that is creative and primordial, willed and filled with meaning, and which cannot be separated from His eternal will.

We might have supposed that God works at two levels, pursuing two disparate objectives: the ontic and the ethical. However, the principle of the unity of God precludes such a conception. The cosmic pattern is identical with the ethical. One absolute will reveals itself both in the cosmic law and in the ethical norm, in physical causation and spiritual motivation. The creative "And God said" of Genesis and the legislative "And God spoke to Moses" represent one will and constitute an identical law; the ethico-cosmic. In short, the natural law is an ethical law, and the whole cosmos is one great ethical drama in the guise of a mathematico-relational and concrete sensuous process. The moral norm and the cosmic necessity are two images of the same universe.

The cosmos, in its seemingly mechanical, insensate, repetitious conformity to the mathematical cycle, is not engaged in a monotonous and absurd performance. It is rather committed to a great undertaking, the realization of the Divine will, which in its very essence is ethical. The cosmic event is an ethical event, hidden, of course, from the human eye which stares only upon the surface and is incapable of apprehending and comprehending the mysterious link between the factual and the meaningful. Naked facticity, stripped of meaning and worth, was never created by God.

"God saw all that He had made, and it was very good" (Gen. 1:31). This predication of the world, that it is good, attests to its ethical design and plan. Otherwise the attribute of good could not be applied. "To be" means to fulfill the Divine will, which manifests itself in the dynamics of Being. The bird in its flight, the flower opening its leaves towards the sunlight, the tumbling pebbles, the sea waves transmitting energy, all these, whether driven by a mechanical force, a biological impulse, or an instinctive drive, carry out a Divine ethical command. They are automatically engaged in the great universal task: the realization of the Divine will that is inherent in them. They can never violate this ethical norm, for they cannot transcend the natural law. Freedom of action was denied to them. Therefore, they do not act, but let themselves be acted upon by the prospective causal law. Yet, the latter secures its force because of the ethical substance.

Kabbalat ol malkhut Shamayim, accepting the yoke of Heaven, signifies the fulfillment of both the natural law and moral law. When we pronounce *Ehad* ("One") and affirm the unity of God, we intend to state that God, in his dual role as Creator and Legislator, Master of the universe and Teacher, is one. His word made heaven and earth spring into existence, and the same word founded the moral law. Hence, the ontic law is moral. Hermann Cohen was wrong in his theory that Judaism did not discover God in the cosmic process and preferred the ethical approach to the ontic. Judaism found God both in the cosmos and in the conscience, in natural and in moral necessity.

Moreover, Judaism uncovered oneness in both realms—the cosmic and the conscience. The cosmic will is neither an antithetic will, running in an opposite direction, nor even a parallel will, running in the same direction to that of the ethical will. One will expresses itself via two media—the cosmos and the apocalypse, the natural law and the moral law. Revelation, however meta-logical and meta-physical as an encounter of God and man, discloses the identical message written in the movement of stars and ocean waves, in the circling of the moth about the light, and the rhythmic pulsating of the human heart. Revelation is the supernatural reconstruction of the Divine will, as an expression of the religious ethos, out of the natural, seemingly neutral and indifferent will of the Creator.

If we should employ the term "transcendental" where we earlier spoke of the ethical order, we would obtain a very important equation: the cosmic order is identical with the transcendental. One pattern runs through the whole of Being, concrete and abstract, natural and supernatural, this-worldly and other-worldly, cosmic-causalistic and spiritual-purposive, mechanical and meaningful. Being as such, on all levels, and in all its manifestations, is one; it reveals God. Unity of God reveals itself in unity of Being, both cosmic and transcendental.

Ontic Unity, not Unity of Substance

Here we arrive at one of the greatest of all Jewish ideas, which we may rightly call the metaphysic of the Exodus. When Moses encountered God in the burning bush and inquired as to the name of the One whose message of redemption he was commanded to bring to the people, he received the cryptic answer, *Ehyeh asher Ehyeh* (Ex. 3:14). Whatever the translation of these words—Philo was the first one to introduce this idea of Divine ontism—Maimonides defined the meaning unequivocally, "I am Being as such" (*Guide* I:63). God's essence is Being; of God it is to be predicated that He is not accidental or adjectival, but necessary and essential; *essentia* and *esse* are identical concerning God. The judgement "God exists" is not only a statement of *essentia* but also of *esse*. It identifies God as being per se. There is no other Being besides You.

> Then God taught Moses how to teach them, and how to establish amongst them the belief in the existence of Himself, namely, by saying *Ehyeh asher Ehyeh...* The first noun which is to be described is *ehyeh*; the second, by which the first is described, is likewise *ehyeh*, the identical word, as if to show that the object which is to be described and the attribute by which it is described are in this case necessarily identical. This is, therefore, the expression of the idea that God exists but not in the ordinary sense of the term; or in other words, He is "the existing Being which is the existing Being" that is to say, the Being whose existence is absolute (*Guide*, I:3, Friedlander translation, 94-95).

In this passage, Maimonides formulates the idea of existing in God. Since He is the absolute Being, no other existence is possible without sharing His Being. Every existence is a relative one and as such must be related to the absolute one; otherwise the relative would become absolute. This relatedness is not that of effect to cause, however permanent it is, but of all-inclusiveness. Since God is the only Being and since this excludes all other things from having a reality of their own, it follows that only in God may one find the completeness of being. "To be" means to participate in the Divine Being; it means "to be in Him."

The paradox of creation thus becomes almost an absurdity. The world was created as a separate substance, but not, however, as a separate existence. Finitude is to be found within infinity, temporality within eternity; the world within God. Creation is an act of tolerance on the part of God; He bestowed grace upon something by allowing it to share his reality. God received the world into His "lap;" in so doing He made its existence possible. Creation is bounded in and enclosed within.

> Scripture accordingly says, "by the life of Pharaoh" and "by the life of thy soul" but not, "by the life of the Eternal," but rather "as God liveth," [or God's life]. Because the Creator and His life are not dual, as is the case with the life of living bodies or the life of angels. Hence too, God does not apprehend creatures and knew them because of them, as we know them. Rather He knows them because of Himself. Therefore, knowing Himself, He knows everything, for everything is attached to Him, in His Being (*Hilkhot Yesodei ha-Torah* 2:10).

However, this doctrine is a far cry from pantheism, whether in its Spinozistic-cosmic or neo-Platonic mystical perspective. Pantheistic philosophies of all schools said that God and world are identical as to their substance. They decreed the oneness of God and world as substance, either by identifying them completely (Spinoza) or by letting the infinite substance of God emanate the finite substances through a multiple phase process. Judaism, by contrast, always declared the incommensurability of God and world as substances. Seen from this perspective, God is at an infinite distance from His creation. The latter is not enclosed by God, but finds itself outside of Him. Yet shifting the categorical approach from substantia to existentia, from matter and content to ontic modality, the whole perspective changes. The world suddenly makes the great leap and discovers itself within Him, enveloped by the Infinite.

Moreover, pantheism reduced Divinity to created reality, be it cosmic or transcendental. The cosmic exhausts itself in its manifestation. Spinoza found only the infinite natural substance, and declared it to be deity, manifesting itself through the mathematical arrangement of nature. There is nothing, according to Spinoza, beyond the concrete-natural world. Plotinus, though he spoke of the One, as the great Beyond, the fountainhead of the multifarious, did not see it as real. Plotinus's One is more of a principle than a reality. Although Judaism admits the immanence of God in His creation and the ontic fellowship of the earth with Him, it insists upon the full absolute transcendence of God in His mystic infinity, and on the complete detachment of God from the creation. The world is thus reduced to the status of existential tenancy: it exists in God, by Him, and shares his reality, not claiming any ontic autonomy. God, however, is absolute and unconditioned. He is all-inclusive; yet He is also all-exclusive, remote and inaccessible. Since God and being are synonymous, and the transcendental world is not an exception to this rule, we must assume that both the cosmic and the transcendental existence merge into one ontic order whose abode is God.

From this metaphysical viewpoint, the unity of God has the connotation of uniqueness, singularity. "God is one" means also that He is the only One who exists, besides whom no other form or manner of autonomous Being is possible. *Ehad* means that God and reality are identical. To exist is tantamount to abiding in God; it means to share his infinite Being, to be with Him and to merge ontically, not substantially, with infinity. *Ehad* is a negating statement, a philosophy of complete nihilation concerning both the world of facts and the world of transcendent existence. Neither exists except in relatedness to God, *Ehyeh Asher Ehyeh*. The root *HVH* (from which the word *Ehyeh* and the Tetragrammaton derive) expresses this idea of Divine Pan-ontic-theism.

Yet creation has been made possible only because God permitted finitude to participate in Being, to attach itself to and possess Him. This is the mystery of *Elokim*, the instrument of Divine creative action. The first verse of *Shema* proclaims not only a theological principle, but an ontic-metaphysical one as well. God-as-being is one, to the exclusion of any other form of reality. Through the grace bestowed upon finitude, the creation is privileged to possess Him as *Elokim* and by so doing, it may lay claim to existence, to reality. Here are two main phases of the God experience. God is one in the sense of exclusiveness and He is one in the sense of all-inclusiveness. This motif is the central theme of *Yotzer Or*, the first *berakhah* preceding the morning *Shema*, a liturgical correlate of the first section of the *Shema* itself.

The Two Themes of Yotzer Or

A thorough examination of the first *berakhah* affords a striking instance of the way historians have misunderstood the central motif of accepting the yoke of Heaven and hence made specious deductions as to the unity of the text. They were perplexed by the transition, which is *prima facie* unwarranted, from the opening, *"ha-Meir la-aretz,"* "He who gives light to the world," to the angelic service. In the first part, the central motif is that of the Divine wisdom expressing itself in the cosmic order, particularly in the rising and setting of the sun—to the naked eye of the observer a most outstanding and magnificent cosmic event. Suddenly, this theme is suspended and a new one is introduced—not one of this-worldly orderliness but of otherworldly vision: the angelic choirs, singing numinous hymns at the very throne of glory, are beheld by the worshipper. Only a moment ago the worshipper glorified God in the simple manner of the psalmist, citing the marvels of nature; now he finds himself in the angelic world of bliss immersed in the magnificence and splendor of something mysterious, awe-inspiring and transcendental. The worshipper, overcome by ecstasy, and filled with solemnity and devotion, joins with the angels to chant the praise of God in the *Kedushah* (sanctification).

It is for this reason that the *Kedushah*, in which the enthusiasm of the visionary culminates, has been introduced into the benediction of *Yotzer Or*. Realistic observation and apprehension of the rationality, simplicity and beauty of nature, on the one hand, and a mystical-ecstatic vision of the numinous beatitude of an apocalyptic order, on the other hand, serve as the double motifs of *Yotzer ha-Meorot*.

Historians failed to find consistency in this change of motifs and concluded that the mystical motif is a later addendum, which goes back only to the fifth century. The original text of the first blessing, according to this view, consisted exclusively of the first theme, dealing with the cosmic event of sunrise and sunset. In order to justify this viewpoint, they attempted to reinterpret, by a *tour de force*, a passage in the Palestinian Talmud which mentions the *Kedushah* of *Yotzer Or* (*Yerushalmi Berakhot* 5:3).

In view of our analysis, the whole structure of *birkat Yotzer Or* appears in a different light; the gap is bridged and the discrepancy is eliminated. Let us examine the basic pattern of this liturgical creation. The opening sentence, "who forms light and creates darkness, makes peace and creates all" quotes, with a minor modification, a phrase from Isaiah 45:7. The prayer connects the cosmic order with an ethical category: God is the Creator of light and darkness, the Maker of peace and all things. The word *ha-kol*, "all," means not only the tangible natural phenomena but ethical ideas as well.

Ha-kol, in this context, serves as a substitute for *ra*, evil, the expression originally used by the prophet. Indeed, the word *ha-kol* offers an explanation of the phrase "creates evil," in Isaiah. *Ra*, evil, is only an illusion, a non-being which one apprehends when beholding only a minute segment of creation. It is a phenomenon isolated from the whole, seen in a limited perspective, which might impress us as impervious to the ethical good. Yet within the greater all-inclusive perspective, embracing the totality of being, it is part of an organic whole. Evil is dissolved into the universal pattern of goodness.

The Midrash quotes a saying of Rabbi Meir who interpreted the phrase *tov me'od* ("very good") in Genesis 1:31 as if it read *tov mavet*, death is good (*Genesis Rabbah* 9:5). The passage we are discussing is to be understood in the same manner. God beheld "all that He had created," creation as a whole, all phenomena in their indissoluble relatedness and compresence, I might say in their full harmony, and therefore He did not apprehend evil. Even death, the most horrible and vicious fiend, has found its rehabilitation.

Maimonides, in his theodicy, availed himself of the same idea:

> Consequently the true work of God is all good, since it is existence. The book which enlightened the darkness of the world says therefore, "And God saw everything that he had made, and, behold it was very good." Even the existence of this corporal element, low as it in reality is, because it is the source of death and all evils, is likewise good for the permanence of the universe and the continuation of the order of things, so that one thing departs and the other succeeds. Rabbi Meir therefore explains the words "and behold it was very good"; that even death was good in accordance with what we have observed in this chapter (*Guide* III:10, Friedlander translation, 266-267).

The following verse, referring to God, confirms this thesis: "Who forms light and creates darkness, makes peace and creates evil; I, God, make all these" (Isaiah 45:7). Here the prophet combines the creation of nature with the creation of ethical values. He does not discriminate between fact and ideal, between the existential and axiological situations. Creation is an all-encompassing act. One will is manifest both in the fact and in the value, in the existent and in the valid. One must not see the physical universe as separated from the realm of the just, the good, and the beautiful. Ethico-axiological realization is the main affair of the universe. The latter is not neutral or indifferent to the normative and moral. It incarnates the Divine ethical will.

This prophetic philosophy found expression in the first section of *Yotzer Or*. The miracle of perennial creation manifests Divine infinite goodness and grace. There is continuous creative action on the part of God, and His engagement must *eo ipso* be an ethical one, since there is no neutral area within the Deity. God is good; whatever he does must have axiological significance. Majesty of God, His glory, wisdom and might, blend perfectly with His grace and kindness. In short, the first motif in *Yotzer Or* is committed to the unity of the Divine will as a cosmic potency and ethical authority. Since the natural law is the guise under which the Divine moral will addresses itself to creation, and the unity of high spiritual value and tangible cosmic occurrence is assured, the concrete order merges with the transcendental.

What is the transcendental order if not an ontic dimension within which the Divine will, personal, explicit and unmasked, is realized in a straightforward, simple and comprehensible manner, in contradistinction to the circuitous, delicate and intricate path which is chosen by the same will in its for quest realization in the cosmic order? The difference is only one of appearance and method. Yet, the Divine will itself appears in both, in the cosmic drama, inscrutable, remote and hidden, too delicate and subtle to be recognized, and in the transcendental world, near and intimate, its meaning open and clear. The same will manifests itself in both orders. That is why the second section is devoted to the angels who personify the pure will in its full simplicity and exactness. Both the stars, acted upon by mechanical forces, and the angels, motivated by love and awe of God, are instruments of the absolute ethico-cosmic will.

God's will includes the entirety of creation. Since it is a creative dynamic will, one that seeks realization and fulfillment through both the kingdom of nature and the kingdom of history, we may say that at this juncture religious thought takes the liberty of transcending the boundary line of theology and entering the epistomologico-metaphysical domain.

❧ *Accepting the Yoke of Heaven*

Let us enumerate some components of accepting the yoke of Heaven, which is, as we have seen, so central to the *Shema*. First, one acknowledges God as the highest and greatest worth in his life; the valid is cherished as such. Second, in the axiological awareness, a normative component emerges: that is to say, one experiences normative pressure, one yearns to realize or to possess its value. Third, we have the fulfillment of the norm: the attainment of the value, the experience of benefit, asserts itself in a continuous compresence, and inseparability, of value and valuing subject.

In the field of religious experience the fulfillment signifies real fellowship of God and man. This ideal is realized via the medium of *Elokim*, Divine immanence within the cosmic drama, which is a fourth component of the experience we are describing. Divine immanence, as we have seen in the previous chapter, spells the unity of the natural and moral law, of the concrete and transcendental order, the unity of creation expressing the Divine moral will.

Ontic monism constitutes a fifth element. Plurality of being is a pagan idea. There is only one form of reality, God. He and Being are identical. Creation is the inclusion of other finite substances and phenomena into the infinite Divine Being. The world, the real and the ideal, the concrete and the transcendental, exist in Him. *Ehad*, unity, signifies that only God exists; nothing else beside Him and besides Him. Only within Him is existence thinkable. *Ehad* means negation of the ontic autonomy of finite creation separated from God.

Love and Separability

At this point, the problem of the inseparability of creature from Creator becomes an epistemological normative challenge. Existence is not a factum but a task, a mission. Real being is possible only within Divine enclosure. One must exist in God, share His infinity and absoluteness. To entreat God is synonymous with apprehending and comprehending the real essence of being. To realize God as the highest value, to attain Him, to possess Him, is to realize one's own being, to possess one's own existence and to reconstitute and reform it. If I possess my own self as a moral being, I am conscious both of my being an integral part of a great process through which the Divine will is realized, in which the cosmic and transcendental order is involved, and I am also conscious of my role as an individual, personal, unique reality, with an intricate task and high meaning; I am then *eo ipso* partaking of God, of *Elokim*, He who, within me, has set a task and it is this task within which I find myself. In short, realization of God as a value is identical with self-realization and self-redemption. The highest norm-realization of the God ideal finds a practical equation; to be.

Under this monistic aspect, we may grasp the great secret of the love of God. Love, which asserts itself in a feeling of possessiveness, of inseparability from the beloved person, is basically an expression of ontic unity, of existential compresence and community. We have earlier developed the dual idea of oneness: we have spoken of substantial unity and existential unity. While pantheism preached the unity of God and world because of their identity of substance, Judaism, insisting upon substantial sep-arateness and incommensurability, preaches ontic monism and oneness.

Let us, by way of illustration, consider the embryo within the mother's womb and the infant after birth. As long as the fetus forms a part of the mother's body, the awareness of identity of mother and child consists in the feeling of unity connected to the dynamics of organic metabolic processes. These phenomena are classified under the heading of substance and accidents. After the child's birth, which entails complete separation from the mother's organism and the attainment of organic functional independence, this feeling of oneness disappears. However, the bond of unity between mother and child is not weakened by organic separation. On the contrary, it is strengthened and becomes indissoluble, the more seemingly independent the child becomes, and the less he needs the assistance of his mother. The great parental love is steeped, not in the manifestation of a pri-mordial instinctive impulse, as is the case in the animal king-dom, not in some form of dependence, but in a higher feeling of spiritual integration, in other words, in a feeling of ontic unity. The child is part of the mother's life, where life does not mean an organic process, but conscious meaningful existence. The child attains centrality; the mother's life revolves about her child. She sees herself in him, she lives for him, and lets him not only share her personal existence but also absorb it. An ontic community is formed which spells oneness of existence.

The meaning of love is precisely this idea of ontic insepara-bility. I love because I feel that in this is my existence warrant-ed, worthwhile and relevant; I love insofar as my existence is attached to and integrated into another existence. The conative element in the love-feeling demonstrates the ontic urge in man, the conscious yearning for a full and perfect personal reality. Love is a response to the norm "thou shalt be." It is the great endeavor on the part of man to realize himself by rehabilitating his personality, from being as factum to being as actus.

In this sense must we understand the love of God. The incessant pursuit of an allegedly ever-fugitive objective springs from a troubled and disquieted personality. Man is restless and insecure because he himself cannot legitimize his ontic status, since he has none of his own. We long to anchor our existences in the absolute and unconditional, in Being as such. We cannot love in our existential vacuum; we must obtain the unequivocal assurance that we exist.

However paradoxical the Cartesian equation of existence and thinking (implied by the proof of my existence through the inference from "I think" to "I am") might appear to us, it reflects a grave and perplexing problem. The only erroneous element in Descartes' formulation of the question, from our point of view, is the epistemological emphasis that he placed upon it, since epistemologically we do not have to be provided with any indirect evidence that we exist. The evidence that I exist is intuitive and immediate rather than discursive and circuitous. Yet metaphysically the problem is very acute. Many a time I question my own existence and ask myself whether I exist. Can I call myself a reality, since death is going to obliterate it completely? Am I entitled to lay claim to ontic worth and relevance, when existence is, so to say, granted to and imposed upon me? Can factum be termed existence? Existence is a noun, which stems from the verb "to exist." If the action is absent how can the result be present? Only by acting does one attain existence. And his action, his loving of God, signifies partaking of His Being: all created things are existentially and necessarily referred to God, not only as their end, but as their ontic root and foundation. This activity of being constantly referred to God is the eternal quest for God that is inscribed in the substance of all things.

Natural and Human Quest for God

We are familiar with the Aristotelian-Maimonidean explanation of circular movement. In their opinion and contrary to classical physics, this process was considered primordial, in their opinion. In the *Guide*, Maimonides' discusses the problem of indirect action by God through the movement of the spheres.

> The circular motion of the sphere is consequently due to the action of some idea which produces this particular kind of motion; but as ideas are only possible in intellectual beings, the heavenly sphere is an intellectual being... We have thus shown that both the soul, the principle of motion, and the intellect, the source of the ideas, would not produce motion without the existence of a desire for the object of which an idea has been formed. It follows that the heavenly sphere must have a desire for the ideal, which it has comprehended, and that ideal, for which it has a desire, is God, exalted be His name! When we say that God moves the spheres, we mean it in the following sense: the spheres have a desire to become similar to the ideal comprehended by them. This ideal, however, is simple in the strictest sense of the word, and not subject to any change or alteration, but constant in producing everything good, while the spheres are corporeal; the latter can therefore not be like this ideal in any other way, except in the production of circular motion; for this is the only action of corporeal beings that can be perpetual (*Guide* II:4, Friedlander translation, 156-157).

We may dispense with this theory as a physical, formal explanation of the motion of the planets, since almost everything said here in this conjunction is obsolete and irrelevant. Maimonides, like other great minds in the Middle Ages, did not grasp the mechanical force operating in nature, since the prominent mentors, from whom they derived their understanding, failed to comprehend the rational-mathematical structure of the universe. Yet, the metaphysical implication of the modern theory is enormous. In place of the medieval idea of spheres endowed with intelligence, we recognize that all things tend of their own spontaneity toward God, the abode of absolute existence, by the power of the mechanical law, which is integrated with the very substance of things.

What appears to us as a mechanical force, as a mathematical formula, might well be an expression of the quest for being, for self-realization. With inanimate things or even in the biological realm, in plants and in animals, which are unendowed with ethical awareness, the quest is to be accounted for as a quest devoid of intention and conscious effort. These things or organisms submit mechanically to the force. For them the drive is a fact, not an action. There is a quest on their part, but not conscious love.

In the human world, however, this quest for God becomes a conscious effort, a meaningful movement towards the attainment of self-being, which is Divine Being. Man seeks himself by seeking his own personality and reality. He is bound to find God; love of God means love of Being. The lover, without the beloved, feels helpless, miserable, lonely. For in love there is mutual partaking of each other's existence. Desertion by the beloved is tantamount to loss of ontic worthiness or the frustration of one's cardinal desire, the desire to be—by denying it steadfastness and legitimacy. In the final analysis, we encounter a new equation, namely: the axiological experience is basically identical with the metaphysico-ontic consciousness. To experience a value, to undertake the great venture of realization and possession, translates itself into the metaphysical act of self-realization within the ontic dimension of attaining self-worth and existential dignity, of ascertaining my own status as a *being*.

All levels of value, however, appear to man as something absolute and final in the ontic sense. Therefore, man, who can easily deceive himself as to the true essence of being, might accept a relative value as a substitute for the *ontos on*, the real Being. One person finds ontic assurance in intellectual exercise, the other in beauty, yet another by indulging in the lover's plea-sures. All of them are seeking just one objective—Being. However, because of short-sightedness, ignorance or sheer stu-pidity, they mistake finitude for infinity, vanity for absolute-ness, and fail to ascertain the identity of what they are seeking. A Hasidic rabbi once said that even the sinner seeks God. The sinner's tragedy lies only in the fact that in his search for God he has wandered off in the wrong direction.

Hence, the quest for God is common to all things, either in the form of a mechanical force, or as a conscious desire for com-pleteness of Being. The idea of ontic monism is the motto of cre-ation as a whole. The quest is found within nature; love is ascer-tainable within man in general. There is no need to formulate a new norm that would stimulate or impel man to love God. What is required is a directive as to the ways and means through which man may find ontic shelter. We lack a compass that would guide us along the uncharted lanes of the world of values and facts, in order to protect us from drifting with the powerful tide away from one's destination.

Love of God and Redemptive Halakhic Action

The verse "And thou shalt love thy God" expresses the idea of perfecting an intelligent love, intentional in its grasp, clear and exact as to direction and means of execution. Here we return to the role of Talmud, the content of Halakhah, which Maimonides introduced into the experience of the worship of the heart (Sefer ha-Mitzvot, Positive Commandment 5). The essence of the Halakhah exhausts itself in one theme: the guidance of man in his metaphysical quest of God, which is eo ipso a yearn-ing for Being as such.

How can one be, in the sense of being that makes it an active participle, which partakes of the active verb, which is more than merely a factum noun? Here, Judaism proclaimed to the world a philosophy of existentialism thousands of years before

Kierkegaard or other modern prophets of this brand of philosophy. Yet what makes Judaism so singular, is not only its priority but also the quality of its approach.

What is the methodical principle employed by Judaism in its venture to find fullness of Being in God? Man was charged with the most paradoxical of missions, the rehabilitation of nature. By this we mean a mission that becomes part of a well-planned, thought-out effort in the direction of ontic self-identification with God. We have already pointed out that the longing for God, and the tending toward Him, is not something exclusively human. All things are directed, through their own inner necessity, toward God because God's cosmic will is engraved into their substances; only in Him do they exist. The only difference between them and man lies in the element of purposive action. While man is active in his quest of God, other things tend automatically towards Him.

Man is a strange phenomenon in the universe. His duality makes him distinct. He is both mechanical nature and conscious personality, unconscious drive and willful anticipation. Hence, he is commissioned to overcome this conflict, and to integrate the insensate in the meaningful, the natural quest into the knowledgeable and willed act.

Here Judaism displayed unlimited ingenuity. Other religions have always been at a loss when confronted with the indisputable fact that man is a member of the animal family and that he has much in common with other biological creatures. Judaism evolved a distinctive approach. The general religious philosophy of man recognized only two alternatives in dealing with man's relation to nature: asceticism or hedonism. Pagan philosophies advocated hedonism. They affirmed in an unqualified manner the instinctual drive of man and his role as an orgiastic voluptuary. Abandonment to the most vulgar pleasures has been compared to a religious performance. Thus, Bacchanalian rites and all kinds of cultic obscenities formed a part of the pagan ritual. On the other hand, Christianity inverted this axiological approach; it preached complete asceticism and renunciation of the bodily self. One serves God with the spirit alone. The body cannot be harnessed to spiritual service.

In contradistinction to both paganism and Christianity, Judaism proposed a third alternative. The body, which harbors in itself the inner necessity of being directed toward God, can and must be redeemed by the intelligence, in such a manner that it might participate in the willfully directed yearning for God as Being, who is at once their root and goal. The bodily functions should cease to be merely diabolic processes, biological tensions and relaxations, moving viciously towards the inevitable exhaustion and destruction of the organism. Instead they become filled with ontic worthiness and relevance, they are referred and related to the central part of the conscious personality for feeling and completeness of being. Judaism does not preach forgetfulness of the body, but, on the contrary, constant watchfulness and remembrance. Judaism did not condemn the hedonic moments in human life if they fit into the general religious frame of reference. Redemption of nature in man is the most outstanding task of the religious personality. The whole of man, body and spirit, nature and consciousness, must be engaged in the love of God, in the clear quest for Being.

"And thou shalt love the Lord your God with all thy soul." The word "all" (*u-ve-khol*) conveys a central thought. In his search for Being man discovers his completeness. He is moved and guided by intelligent planning; he rids himself of ethical indifference. There are no more neutral areas in his existence from which the halakhic ethical norm is barred. The concrete person (not an abstract entity) commits himself totally to God-Being. Through this commitment man finds the oneness of Being in which he shares.

In our discussion of the unity of God, the realization of which entails a practical commitment leading even to martyrdom, we have already seen how Judaism's ethical emphasis affects our general way of life, as philosophical understanding gives birth to all-embracing self-sacrifice. In the present analysis we have discovered how Judaism unites the natural and intellectual aspects of the human being. The philosophical scope of the consequences is enormous, even on a purely axiological level. The Judaic idea of nature confirms the practical set of ideas we encountered earlier. Because the Jew saw the natural order as the work of the Creator, he never experienced the great and perplexing problem of the tragic which is accompanied by despair, concerning a life which is devoid of any absolute meaning at all and which is not man's free creation at all. Existence was, indeed, imposed upon him: "Against your will do you live" (*Avot* 4:21). If existence is an ethical ideal, and a value whose realization moves from confined and limited concreteness toward the ontic vastness and boundlessness of reality, then the tragic becomes the heroic effort, the great adventure of self transcendence. The nonsensical becomes grandiose; the indifferent, relevant and meaningful; suffering, a sacrifice. When life is factum, death is tragic. When life is action, death is great.

Since, for Judaism, the worthy life is defined not only through noetic achievement but also by ethical endeavor, one does not have to be a Socrates or a Kant in order to live a full life. The Greeks reduced true existence to the theoretical life (*bios theoretikos*); logos was employed as the only means of lending worth to man. Living in a dignified and worthwhile manner became the exclusive privilege of the few, whom Providence favored with an intellectual talent. Judaism, always impervious to religious esotericism, has made it possible for all to have a full life. Judaism devised another medium through which man can realize himself and attain true ontic relevance—the normative halakhic method. Life in all its dimensions becomes an ethical affair, exoteric and simple.

The way to the metaphysical ontic experience is via the ethico-halakhic domain. Existence is to be comprehended not only in contemplative noetic but also in halakhic categories. As a matter of fact, the cognitive method, though very helpful in promoting the betterment of our physical environment, cannot assist man in his search for ontic worth and meaning in life. Knowledge on a relational formal level, knowledge of the causal links in the mechanical chain of phenomena, does not endow man with the axiological understanding of its meaningfulness. On the contrary, one-sided preoccupation with that kind of knowledge makes living a more baffling and irrational affair. The only way to endure, with the mystifying quality that makes living a worthwhile engagement, does not lead through abstract knowing but through partaking of and involving oneself in life with a specific ethical intention. One lives by giving meaning to life, by relating it to something beyond it. The task of Halakhah is to sanctify nature.

❧ *Reflections on the Amidah*

Redemption, *ge'ulah*, is one of the most fundamental ideas of Judaism. It is not confined to the national-historical spheres, but extends over the diverse domains of existence.

Everything requires redemption: the historical community, the individual, nature, the world as whole—all cry out for redemption and repair. In similar fashion, man's thoughts, ideas, reflections, ideals and feelings must be redeemed. All these find themselves in narrow straits; they all cry out to God to be made explicit.

Even the *Shekhinah*, the Divine Presence, as it were, is a captive of historical and metaphysical exile and hopes for redemption.

Sometimes an idea remains forlorn and anonymous within a system of thought until its redeemer comes, extricating it from loneliness and desolation, liberating it, and bringing it to a position of centrality. Just as the Redeemer [the Messiah] whom we all await will lift the impoverished nation from the ashes, so, too, is the spiritual redeemer sent to mend an idea and establish it in its glory and grandeur. The history of human thought is replete with examples, and there is no need to cite them. There is a commonly repeated expression: "My ancestors left me

---

Endnotes to this chapter are on p. 182—*Ed.*

an area to fence in" or "God has left me an area" (*Hullin* 7a). What does this mean?

Halakhic thought, too, is subject to redemption. Some halakhic concepts were sentenced to a long or short period of exile, and strove for redemption over the generations until the advent of their redeemer—one of the sages of Israel who was selected by Providence to bring those concepts out of isolation and into the center of halakhic thought. Suddenly, an anonymous idea, which had been hidden away in a corner, begins to move from the periphery to the center, from concealment to revelation.

One halakhic concept that was sentenced to temporary isolation but was at last redeemed, is *avodah she-ba-lev* (service, or worship, of the heart). The concept of *avodah she-ba-lev* was coined by the Talmudic sages.[1] The Tosafists, for example, cite a Rabbinic text on Deut. 11:13: "To serve Him with all your heart—what is the service of the heart? That is to say prayer" (*Ta'anit* 2a). But despite this derivation from a Biblical verse, prayer was regarded as a rabbinic commandment and did not occupy a central place in halakhic thought. Many discussed prayer, and many laws were formulated about it. Yet the central point, prayer as service of the heart, awaited its redeemer, who would highlight it and fill it with content. Providence eventually ordained that the redeemer appear.

Rambam on the Status of Prayer

The first redeemer of prayer was Rambam (Maimonides). Thus ordained the Master of the universe, omniscient Diety. Rambam restored to prayer its crown, its preeminent position known to us from the days of the Patriarchs and prophets. Although both his and his opponents' views are "the words of the living God" [*Eruvin* 13b], yet it was Rambam who merited being the restorer.

Rambam's contribution in the area of prayer is revolutionary in two respects. First of all, he determined as a matter of practical halakhah that prayer is a Biblical commandment—contrary to the virtual halakhic consensus, a view taken as almost obvious, that the obligation to pray every day is only rabbinic. Secondly, he held that prayer is identical with service of the heart, an idea that is, according to Rambam, all-encompassing and all-pervasive and which represents the essence of man's relationship with God.[2] This great halakhic achievement and philosophical innovation has become a basic principle of our world view, both in halakhic thought and in the religious experience of our people.

Ramban (Nahmanides), in trying to defend those of Rambam's predecessors who did not regard prayer as a Biblical commandment, found it necessary to admit that, despite the absence of a fixed law obligating daily prayer, the substance of prayer and its essence are derived from the Torah.[3] In times of distress, he admitted, there exists a Biblical obligation upon the community to cry out and beseech the God of Israel. In effect, Ramban's concession mitigates his absolute position that prayer is not a Biblical obligation at all. Actually, it was Rambam who also introduced the idea of the singular importance of prayer in time of trouble and distress (*Hilkhot Ta'anit* 1:1-2). He was the first to identify the commandment of blowing the trumpets [Num. 10:9] with the commandment to plead and cry out.

According to Rambam, it is impossible to conceive of Divine worship without including prayer in it. What then is prayer? It is the expression of the soul that yearns for God via the medium of the word, through which the human being gives expression to the storminess of his soul and spirit.

The Torah commands love and fear of God, total commitment to Him and cleaving unto Him. Antithetical, dynamic experiences which seek to erupt and reveal themselves must be integrated into the external, concrete realm through the forms of language and expression, by means of song, weeping and supplication.

Had the Torah not commanded prayer as the exclusive medium for expressing inward worship—we do not know what the

God-seeking human being, whose soul thirsts for the living God, would do. Could one entertain the thought that Judaism would want man to suppress his experience? On the contrary! The Halakhah was always interested in expressions of the inner life, in the uncovering of the subjective and opaque, and in the conversion of emotion and thought into action. How could one assume that the Halakhah was totally oblivious to the supreme attainment—that is, to prayer?! Did Halakhah demand that worship be mute, that experiences be concealed, that they not be allowed expression?

When Rambam said that prayer is Biblically ordained and identical with the service of the heart, he thereby redeemed love, fear, and indeed our entire religious life from muteness. They were given a voice. The lover expresses his yearning, the trembler his fear, the wretched and dejected his helplessness, the perplexed his confusion, and the joyful his religious song—all within the framework of prayer. The service of the heart gained a foothold in the world of forms and facts. Experience and prayer constitute two poles between which the great service of God oscillates.

The *act* (ma'aseh) of prayer is formal, the recitation of a known, set text; but the *fulfillment* of prayer, its *kiyyum*, is subjective: it is the service of the heart. The intention (*kavvanah*) required for prayer is not like the *kavvanah* required for other *mitzvot*.[4] In other commandments the intention is not the most important element. It is a secondary element, even if it is required for fulfillment of the *mitzvah*. Rather it is the act, the concrete action, that is primary, and *kavvanah* simply accompanies the action.[5] With prayer, however, *kavvanah* is the essence and substance: prayer without intention is nothing.

Hasidism, which placed so much stress on the spiritual element, the subjectivity in religious life, and which devoted so much attention to the act of prayer and to the individual's coming closer to God through prayer, is also sustained by Rambam's view of *avodah she-ba-lev* as an all-encompassing, all-penetrating experience. Because of Rambam, the concept of prayer became a central element in Jewish thought.

Prayer, which is like a mirror reflecting the image of the person who worships God with heart and soul, is shot through with perplexity, for worship itself is rooted in the human dialectical consciousness. Hence prayer is not marked by monotonous uniformity. It is multi-colored: it contains contradictory themes, expresses a variety of moods, conflicting experiences, and desires oscillating in opposing directions. Religious experience is a multi-directional movement, metaphysically infused. Prayer too does not proceed slowly along one straight path, but leaps and cascades from wondrous heights to terrifying depths, and back.

Sources of Prayer

Let us now examine the fundamental components of the *Amidah*.

Rambam stated as a matter of law that, although the formula and times for prayer are Rabbinic in origin, the threefold structure of prayer is Biblical. The first three benedictions comprise praise (*shevah*); the middle benedictions comprise supplication and petition; and the last three benedictions comprise acknowledgment and thanksgiving. Rambam writes: "Rather this commandment obligates each person to offer supplication and prayer every day and utter praises of the Holy One, blessed be He; then petition for all his needs with requests and supplications; and finally give praises and thanks to God for the goodness that He has bestowed upon him. [He is to do this] each day according to his own ability" (*Hilkhot Tefillah* 1:2).

Needless to say, Rambam derived his position from Talmudic sources. The Rabbis frequently emphasized the importance of the order of prayer, and deduced the formula of prayer from biblical texts. They taught: "May one ask his needs and then pray? Solomon already has stated—'To hearken to the *rinnah* and the *tefillah'* [I Kings 8:28]: *rinnah* is prayer; *tefillah* is petition" (*Berakhot* 31a). Praise of God must precede petition for one's needs, as we learn from another rabbinic statement: "R. Simlai expounded: A man should always recount the praise of the Holy One, blessed be He, then pray. How do we know this? From Moses; for it is written: 'And I entreated God at that time,' and it says, 'You began to show Your servant Your greatness... let me pass over and see the good land' [Deut. 3:23-25]" (*Berakhot* 32a).

For Rambam, these *derashot* (rabbinic deductions of laws from of biblical texts) provide a full-fledged proof that the principles of prayer are derived from the Torah, rather than the Torah verses constituting a mere prop or support (*asmakhta*). The halakhic outlook necessitates this approach. For the Halakhah could not overlook an apparently irresolvable problem and paradox. Relating to God through speech and supplication appears to our sages as a brazen and adventurous activity. How can mortal man, who is today here and tomorrow in the grave, approach the supreme King, the Holy One blessed be He? Does an ordinary subject have license to speak to a great and exalted King and petition Him for his needs?

Of course, the experience of fear and trembling, which is an integral part of religious life, complicates the problem of prayer and turns it into a riddle. On the one hand, it is impossible for man to come close to God. The more he approaches God, the more man negates his finite human status. Finitude is swallowed up by infinity and perishes in its labyrinth. Man at times flees from God and hides from Him, lest he be engulfed: "And Moses hid his face, for he feared to look upon God" (Ex. 3:6). Man's selfhood and self-confidence are annulled in confrontation with the greatness of God and His majesty. If so, the question arises: How can prayer take place? Prayer is standing before God, in the presence of the *Shekhinah;* but how can man find himself in the presence of God without losing his individual existence? God, the awesome and terrifying sovereign, negates all being, annihilates all otherness, and turns all else into nothingness. When Moses pleaded with God to be shown His Glory, he received but a curt reply: "You cannot see My Face, for no man can see Me and live" (Ex. 33:20). When God speaks to him, the prophet recoils and collapses in trembling. Daniel attests to such a psychological state, and Rambam incorporated the latter's description into his code: "When any of them prophesy, their limbs tremble, their physical powers are attenuated, they lose control of their senses, and thus their minds are free to comprehend what they see, as it states concerning Abraham 'and a great dark dread fell over him' (Gen. 15:12). Similarly, Daniel (10:8) states: 'My appearance was horribly changed and I retained no strength'" (*Hilkhot Yesodei ha-Torah* 7:2).[6]

If this is the case, what is the character of prayer? The whole substance of prayer as petition and supplication for man's petty needs, as we have indicated, is puzzling and beyond our ken. Can man attain a foothold within Divine transcendence? Can he shower Him with a plethora of insignificant matters?

Halakhic thought labored mightily to resolve this question and to discover a basis for permitting flesh and blood to approach his Creator. This permission is based on three fundamental ideas of Judaism:

First: as we have explained, prayer is a vital necessity for the religious individual. He cannot conceal his thoughts and his feelings, his vacillations and his struggles, his yearnings and his wishes, his despair and his bitterness—in a word, the great wealth stored away in his religious consciousness—in the depths of his soul. Supressing liturgical expression is simply impossible: prayer is a necessity. Vital, vibrant religiosity cannot sustain itself without prayer. In sum, prayer is justified because it is impossible to exist without it.

Second: Our Rabbis permitted prayer not only because it is impossible for man to exist without it, but because there is historical *precedent* for it. The Patriarchs, Moses and the prophets, all fell before God in supplication, conversing with Him as a man would with a friend, laying bare before Him that which was hidden in their hearts, burdening Him, as it were, with their needs. They argued with Him, even made demands. We can rely on the practice of our nation's Patriarchs, who approached God and strove to attach themselves to Him. Verily, fear causes trembling; yet the historical fact cannot be gainsaid. Prayer is a time-honored institution in Judaism, having been revealed at the very dawn of the nation.

Third: The Temple cult, the offering of sacrifices, is a fundamental ingredient in Halakhah. To bring a sacrifice is to come close to God. The Torah desired that man be intimate with God. Man must not flee from Him, but rather must yearn for and move toward Him. It is in these terms that the sacrificial cult in the Temple must be understood. From time to time, said the Torah, man is to encounter God and stand before Him. He is not to fear being consumed by Infinity and thus ceasing to be. Finite existence is not consumed by the infinite Divine Being. On the contrary, finite being gains strength and power and finds redemption from existential exile. In similar fashion, prayer, too, permits man to confront God. Thus, if bringing a sacrifice constitutes the fulfillment of a *mitzvah*, then prayer, too, is a positive commandment.

The Talmudic dictum "the prayers were established by the Patriarchs" does not contradict a second statement of the Sages, "the prayers were established to correspond to the fixed daily sacrificial offerings, the *temidim*."[7] Rambam quoted both opinions, for they are mutually complementary. Prayer is justified by both factors, historical precedent and the ceremonial law of the Temple cult.

For this reason, Halakhah insisted upon the formality and orderliness of prayer, upon a standardized structure and a set text, and prohibited anarchy and arbitrariness in man's approach to God. Were it not that scriptural passages speak of prayer, we would have no right to pray. For that reason, one should not add to the standard format of prayer.

We know that the Torah commands the offering of two daily sacrifices. Corresponding to these offerings, prayer was ordained by *Anshei Keneset ha-Gedolah*, members of the Great Assembly, for morning and afternoon. The evening prayer was established to correspond to the consumption of the limbs and fatty parts upon the altar. The Patriarchs also prayed at these times. No Jew has the right to add to the three prayers ordained by the sages of Israel; we have no license to compose new prayers. We find in the Talmud: "R. Judah said in the name of Samuel: If someone was standing in prayer and remembered that he had already prayed, he must cease, even in the middle [of the benediction]" (*Berakhot* 21a). It is forbidden to repeat one's recitation of an obligatory prayer. Once is enough! If one adds, it is as if he had offered two of the daily sacrifices.[8] "R. Hiyya bar Abba said: Whoever prolongs his prayer and dwells upon it eventually incurs heartache" (*Berakhot* 32b). We today no longer are competent in the articulation of elective prayer (*nedavah*); hence we do not have such prayers.

When a Jew prays, he must be fastidious about the entire order and form of the prayer. One must begin not with supplication but instead with acknowledgement through praise and song. Only gradually may one pass to the presentation of needs. It would be errant impudence to push forward vulgarly and to press God to respond to our petitions before we have greeted Him with hymns. As the prophets did, so is the law of the Torah.

The Prayerful Stance Before God

That praise precedes supplication and the whispered plea is based on a fundamental motif of religious experience. Man fears God and reveres Him, but also loves Him. Man withdraws from Him but also longs for Him; his soul yearns for the living God. In such a state of mind, he envisions God not only as a lofty and exalted King—standing apart, distinct from all other reality— but as a merciful Father, the source of his being, a shelter and haven for his ruptured and torn soul, a comfort and safe shore for a lonely, forlorn refugee whose ship has been engulfed in a terrifyingly stormy ocean. Man yearns for God, desires to cling to Him and cleave unto Him forever. Man does not feel that Infinity is antagonistic to finitude. To the contrary, God supports and fortifies man's conditioned, limited status.

From the midst of this experience man views God, as it were, like a friend walking among companions: "And Noah walked with God" (Gen. 6:9). Man extrudes the fear and dread, the wondrous and the mysterious, and fills his consciousness with an assured love. The rendezvous [with God] is not an affront, but instead a mutual encounter of friends who dwell securely together, bonded by love. At this stage, man's relationship to God is rooted in the experience of love and is borne of man's observation of nature, creatures and the world as a whole; this gives rise to wonder and reverence, to enthusiasm and exaltation, and to inspiration. This observation is ecstatic. Man experiences God's sublimity and grandeur, His infinity, omnipotence and omniscience, His disclosure in the world through the cosmic drama, through the experience of God's mightiness and majesty, for the universe and all that fills it demonstrate all these. "The heavens tell God's Glory, and the firmament proclaims His handiwork" (Ps. 19:1).

Awareness of God as Creator of the world and of man is a firm principle of Judaism. The Torah opens with "in the beginning," with the world's genesis. From the cosmic experience there is born, as we noted, a love directed toward God. Love of God is thus based on man's relationship to the majestic reality on which the Holy One, blessed be He, has imprinted His seal. Rambam established this as a halakhic principle: "What is the way to attain love and fear of Him? When a person contemplates His wondrous and great deeds and creations and appreciates His infinite wisdom that surpasses all comparison, he will immediately love, praise, and glorify Him, yearning with tremendous desire to know God's great name as David (Ps. 42:3) stated: 'My soul thirsts for the Lord, for the living God'" (*Hilkhot Yesodei ha-Torah* 2:2).

Therefore the Rabbis ordered Israel's tributes (i.e., prayer) so that praise for God's mighty works and wonders bursts forth immediately. Man does not begin with trembling, but by approaching with love, by singing a hymn about the wonders of creation.

Abraham discovered God by observing the universe and all it contains; he was the first to stand before God. Is it possible to stand before God? Indeed it is! Abraham was the one who discovered the secret that man should not flee or hide from the presence of God as Adam did. Man can hold his ground; the creature can appear before the Creator. Abraham brought the message of prayer to the world: man may pour out his feelings before God and have a dialogue with Him. The kingdom of Heaven is filled with inexhaustible lovingkindness. The Holy One, blessed be He, does not insist upon the protocol of His absolute kingship and sovereignty. "Wherever you find God's grandeur, there too you find His humility" [*Megillah* 31a]. God approaches man in lovingkindness and sympathy, which incorporates an element of friendship. The belief that God descends into the world of man as his familiar companion, as one who lives with him in the same abode, is one of the principles upon which the ancient covenant is based. "I will walk with you and dwell in your midst," God proclaims [Lev. 26:12]. In fact, the question we presented above—how is prayer possible—is both a general theoretical question and also a specific practical question. From a theoretical perspective we answered that the possibility of prayer is based on three foundations (pp. 150–51). All the same, every individual who comes to pray grapples anew with this question, as he seeks to initiate the prayer with fearful supplication and petition: his initial, immediate reaction is expressed in paralyzing fear and shuddering dread. How is it possible to set up a dialogue between man and his Creator, he asks himself. As his lips move with trepidation and trembling, he expresses his frailty and nothingness, beginning the *Amidah* as follows: "God, open my lips, let my mouth utter Your praise" (Ps. 51:17). In other words: I do not know how to move my lips, how to find the right words to express the thoughts in my heart. O God, do this on my behalf. I plead with You not only to fulfill my petitions and satisfy my needs, but to guide me regarding the very substance of prayer. I am ignorant, I know nothing. This is the general preamble to prayer: the unfortunate one confesses his lowliness, his grief and his despair. He pleads with God: teach me how to pray! Nonetheless, within the space of a single phrase comes *Avot*, the first benediction of the *Amidah*. God's kingship is not mentioned in this benediction. The Holy One, blessed be He, revealed Himself to Abraham not as King but as Father.

The First Blessing: Avot

Avot contains two elements: that of paternal lovingkindness and the appeal to historical precedent. The Jew who prays sees himself as integrated with those who have carried the burden over the generations, as connected to the past and the future like a link in one long chain. Awareness of historical continuity, strong faith in the messianic, eschatological destiny of the nation, and the experience of attachment to the generations assure the praying person that God will not reject him. The God who walked with Abraham, the God to whom Abraham prayed, the God who forged a covenant with Abraham, will not hide His face from the individual who prays, even though the latter is hapless and unworthy of standing before Him. In the *Avot* benediction, one recites: "He who remembers the *hesed* of the Patriarchs and brings a Redeemer to the children of their children for the sake of His Name with love." The everlasting continuity of the nation guarantees my worth and value in the eyes of God. If sanctity does not inhere in the individual personality *per se*, it nevertheless takes hold of the individual by virtue of his identifying with those generations that struggled for the existence of the nation. On his own, the person who prays is without worth; but in the context of the generations, he reflects the image of Abraham, the father of all generations!

In the benediction of *Avot* one praises God for three of His attributes: great, mighty, and awe-inspiring (*gadol, gibbor, nora*). The Rabbis say: "Had Moses not pronounced these [attributes] in the Torah and had not the men of the Great Assembly ordained this in the prayer, we would be unable to say it" (*Berakhot* 33b). These three attributes represent the transcendental awareness, expressing its three characteristics and tendencies. *Gadol* means full of lovingkindness (*gedulah* and *hesed* are equated). Man senses God by feeling the great emanation of *hesed* that descends upon him; he recognizes the footprints of God in the great world. One who prays appreciates that being able to pray to God whenever he wishes and wherever he is, is the supreme gift of *hesed*: "And I, in the multitude of your *hesed*, enter Your abode" [Ps. 5:8]. This *hesed* gives him the power to approach God, the author of the *hesed*, with words of propitiation and supplication.

The Second Blessing: Gevurot

Man cognizes God in the world not only as abundant in *hesed* but also as *gibbor*, omnipotent. No action lies beyond His capacity. In this experience of Divine mightiness is embedded also man's sense of frailty and helplessness, and from this sensibility there emerges a recognition of utter exhaustion. Man cannot be his own master; he cannot nourish his personality on his own and preserve his independence. He is not free, nor is he able to plan, initiate and execute through his own powers. He requires God's assistance, blessing and supervision. A feeling of waiting for God suffuses the human being. The Divine attribute *gibbor* implies to him that none of his human achievements are the fruit of his thought and action, but only the product of the

Divine act and might. Pride recedes, humility grows. At first man approaches with joy and wholeness of soul, a cleaving unto God who calls out to him from the hidden recesses. This optimistic stance gives way to the cry of one who feels frail and miserable and whose eyes are lifted to "deliverance and rescue from another place" [Esther 4:14]. God abounds in kindness and is also mighty. To this latter attribute the Rabbis devoted a special benediction: *Gevurot*.

In this blessing we describe God as mighty, not only in the sense that the cosmos is dynamic, but in an ethical sense. God is omnipotent and mighty—and hence He is *rav le-hoshi'a*, "the great Savior."

God's might is not concentrated only in the dynamic that governs the cosmic process, but extends into the realm of the moral as well. Mightiness is modeled on *hesed*. God saves those who cannot be delivered and redeemed on their own. All God's deeds, all His acts, even in the realm of nature, are imprinted with an ethical seal. The causal-cosmic process is nothing but an exalted ethical drama, which is rooted in the Divine will that is beyond our grasp. We do not understand how the laws of nature relate to the absolute ethical laws of God. But the bond exists. God's will is the source of ethics and also of natural law. God, who sustains the cosmos, who is consummate in His might, is the possessor of the infinite moral will. The Jew enumerates the mighty acts of God in a specific, singular manner: "Who sustains the living with *hesed*, resurrects the dead with abundant mercy, supports the fallen and heals the sick, releases the confined and maintains his faith with those who sleep in the dust." Here the Jew does not sing about the might of God by reference to the stability of creation, its breadth and greatness, the energy active in it, or the stormy elements that abide within, as did the psalmist: "Thou rulest the raging of the sea: When the waves thereof rise up, Thou stillest them" (89:10); "And He rode upon the Cherub, and did fly: He soared on the wings of the wind" (18:11); "So is this great and wide sea wherein are creeping things innumerable, both small and great beasts" (104:25). The arrangers of the *Amidah* prayer refrained from introducing into the prayer the aesthetic moment, the impact on the soul of the majesty and beauty of creation, the sublimity inherent in it. One who prays the *Amidah* does not recite, "Bless the Lord, O my soul, O Lord my God, Thou art very great, Thou are clothed with glory and majesty" (Ps. 104:1). Such a hymn does not burst forth from the prayer. Those who arranged the prayer introduced the cosmic-majestic element into the *Pesukei de-Zimrah* (the preliminary psalms of the morning service), but not into the *Amidah* prayer. The dynamic and the beautiful of are not the context for this prayer. The ear of the individual at prayer is bent to receive the whisperings of the moral law that is active within the beauty, the moral might found within the splendor of power. The heart of the person at prayer senses the miracle of a moral vision embroidered in the cosmic veil, and he recounts it in his prayer.

The Rabbis were strict with respect to exaltation and praise, permitting only the use of the three attributes mentioned by our teacher Moses—*gadol, gibbor, nora*. We cannot praise the Infinite drawing upon the cogitations of our limited hearts: "What is the meaning of the verse, 'who can express the mighty acts of the Lord, or make all his praise heard' (Ps. 106:2)? For whom is it fitting to express the mighty acts of the Lord? For one who can make all His praises heard. Raba Bar Bar Hana said in the name of R. Yohanan: one who enumerates upon the praise of the Holy One, blessed be He, to excess is uprooted from the world as it says: 'for Thee, silence is praise' (Ps. 65:2)" (*Megillah* 18a). Such statements are scattered throughout the vast Talmudic and Midrashic literature, and they testify to a characteristic sensibility. Although the sages of the Halakhah taught that prayer should begin with praise of God, their minds recoiled from the proliferation of praises and poetry on the part of the person who prays. Only one kind of song to God was allowed, a song that includes not only the eruption of the totality of the creature's yearning, but a pure way of life, a religious-ethical imperative. Because all of creation represents the moral activity of God, and all the processes of cosmic creation serve as conduits for the supreme purposive volition that is enfolded in the cosmic will, aesthetic-ecstatic contemplation turns into an ethical demand—a command to act. You will not find in the Bible any song that does not culminate in ethical conclusions. Even the most sublime hymn on the beauty and splendor ends with a moral judgment: "I will sing praise to my God while I live... I will rejoice in the Lord. Let sinners depart from the earth, and the wicked are no more. Let my soul bless God, Halleluiah" (Ps. 104:33-35).

Rambam formulated a wonderful and pertinent teaching. He maintained that the attributes of Divine action whose use is permitted to man, are all moral principles, imposing upon man an ethical obligation, and compelling him to mend his ways according to the ethical-halakhic imperative which derives from observing the world. We would not have been permitted the most sublime praise of the Deity, if this praise did not obligate us to follow in His ways and to imitate Him.[9]

The blessing of *Gevurot*, then, teaches us how to approach God from an ethical standpoint that we acquire through an understanding of the world. Science reveals to us the might of the Holy One, blessed be He, with respect to the dynamics, energy and mechanical workings of nature. But this initiative alone is not sufficient. The ethical strand inherent in these aspects of nature is to be emulated and imitated. The central commandment of the 613 is to follow the ways of God.

Interesting is the Jewish conception that the greatest of all kindnesses, the singular ethical act, is resurrection of the dead. God involves Himself with the dead, whose existence has already ceased, who not only are unable to act or attain anything, but who are also stripped of the capacity to demand and complain, to plead and entreat, who, having lived, are now consigned to the abyss of the silent grave. The dead person, too, needs deliverance, and God will resurrect the dead. The *hesed* that God performs with the dead is the most miraculous and majestic ethical act. *Gevurot* concludes with repeated reference to the motif of resurrection of the dead. Some spark of this conception is embodied in the halakhah about the obligation to bury a *met mitzvah* (an unattended corpse), which overrides many other commandments; also in the idea that burying the dead constitutes *hesed shel emet* [the *hesed* of truth, because it is offered to one who is unable to repay the kindness].

Third Benediction: Kedushat Ha-Shem

Finally comes the attribute *nora* (awe-inspiring), which symbolizes the pole opposite to that expressed in *Avot*. Awesomeness conveys absolute separation, the absence of any direct relationship between God and man. God is not accessible to the human search, but is rather separated and isolated from it. He cannot be grasped via intellectual comprehension, by way of the experience of the beautiful and the good. From this perspective it is impossible to approach God at all. Since coming closer to God culminates in the annihilation of man, the question arises again: if God appears as the awesome God, how can prayer subsist? Does not the notion of an intimate conversation with the awesome God, who is singular and unique and negates all other being, carry within itself two opposites? How is it possible for the Jew to relate to God as "Thou," when "Thou" nullifies the existence of the praying individual?

Nonetheless, Judaism did not despair of worship of the heart. Even in the realm of the experience of the awesome it wished to attain the impossible and illogical. The praying individual stands and whispers: "You are holy and Your name is holy." The immediate conclusion is that prayer in this mood is an enormous riddle. No human being, no limited, finite creature, can attempt dialogue with the Infinite. Nonetheless, he continues: "And the holy beings each day extol You." There is such a thing as standing before Him, cleaving unto Him; the praying person stands before God, great and awesome. It is in the context of this riddle that the fundamental element of *avodah she-ba-lev* emerges.

Prayer and Sacrifice

The Torah identified religious worship with worship in the *Mikdash* (the Temple). As we indicated above, *avodah* (worship) is a synonym for sacrifice (*hakravah*). The worshipper offers a sacrifice to God. As regards literal sacrifice, the Torah knows only of animal offerings; it bans human sacrifice as practiced by the people of the ancient Near East. But, as we noted, this prohibition applies only to physical sacrifice; when it comes to experiential sacrifice—this God demands from us. Offering an animal is merely a symbolic act. The fundamental correlative of the external action is a spiritual action of self-sacrifice. The blood sprinkled on the altar, the fat and limbs consumed by fire— these represent the blood and fat of the owner of the sacrifice. The inner act of sacrifice is the binding of oneself on the altar. Isaac was the *olah*, the burnt offering set aside for God. In the consciousness of the nation is etched the binding of Isaac as a human sacrifice. His ashes are collected upon the altar. We have no interest in the ram's ashes. Already in childhood we learned the words of Rashi on Leviticus 26:42: "Why does scripture not say that God remembers Isaac? This is unnecessary: for God says, as it were, 'the ashes of Isaac are ever visible before me as though they were heaped upon the altar.'" The ram was offered—but Isaac took on its form and was sacrificed with it. God did not nullify the command of the *akedah*. When he sent His angel to warn Abraham not to lay his hand upon the young man, Abraham already had completed the act of sacrifice. It was fully consummated when he held the knife. The external drama was altered; the inner one remains. Isaac is bound upon the altar, transformed into the ram—a sacrificed ram, whose blood has been sprinkled, whose body has been burned, whose ashes are gathered on Mount Moriah for all generations. The binding of Isaac, which occupies such an important place in Israel's liturgy and world view, means: the binding and sacrifice of man. The doctrine of *korbanot*, of offering to God, demands human sacrifice, but in the form of an animal. Man-spirit, garbed in animal-body, is offered up to God.

After the Temple was destroyed and the daily offerings ceased, the concept of worship remained unaltered. The symbol may be lacking, but the idea survives. Animal sacrifice is not practiced in our day; human sacrifice endures! This principle, that sacrifice comes as a ransom for man who is obligated to offer himself to God, was formulated by R. Abraham Ibn Ezra and Ramban.[10] God demands of man His "deposit," man's being, and man must restore everything to his Owner. The filth of sin precipitates this demand. Soul and body belong to God: "The soul is Yours and the body Your handiwork." The trustee must return to its owner the object entrusted—man's finite being. However, God, in His mercy exchanged one offering for the other, as ransom to God. Yet this substitution pertains only to the physical symbol of the offering. The spiritual act remains in place. The sacrificer binds his body and soul on the altar of the burnt offering, dedicating these to God.[11]

Ramban inquired deeply into the idea of sacrifice, elevating the concept to a sublime mystical height. The requirement to sacrifice flows from the Attribute of Judgment (*middat ha-din*). God demands the human burnt offering. The manifestation of God—awesome and all-powerful—negates a world that is sequestered in the borders of otherness and is content with the relative and the temporal. *Din* jealously guards the absolute uniqueness of God and demands the annulment of finite independent being. God will not tolerate the arrogant man. Man who has become alienated from his Creator through a horrifying ontic pride, must mount the altar of God. The revelation of the *akedah* imperative suddenly erupts from the silent twilight of transcendence, addressing the guardian who has betrayed his task and misappropriated his Master's work.[12]

Build an altar. Arrange the wood. Kindle the fire. Take the knife to slaughter your existence for Me. This is the command of the awesome God who suddenly appears out of an absolute separation. This approach is the very foundation of prayer. Man hands himself over to God. He approaches the awesome God, expressing this movement in sacrifice and binding of oneself.

Structure of the Three Opening Benedictions

The three opening benedictions thus place in relief three fundamental motifs pertaining to the structure of prayer and its essence. First, man yearns for God and discovers Him via that which surrounds him. God is the God of *hesed* who permeates all, and makes the creature a partner in his Being. In Him we find a refuge and stronghold, a protective fortress. We approach Him calmly and confidently. The motto is "Divine *hesed* everlasting," (Ps. 103:17) from the beginning to the end of the generations. The God of Abraham participates in the sorrow of the miserable, impoverished human being. He responds to his entreaty and hears his cry. Unto Him do we pray.

Studies in the psychology of religion that report on the benefit of prayer as a source of consolation and relief for the weary, reflect the belief that the God of *hesed* receives our prayer with love and favor.

The situation is altered when we move from *Avot* to *Gevurot*. Here prayer changes direction. At the outset, in the benediction of *Avot*, the praying individual did not feel confusion, need or inadequacy. At this first stage he lacked nothing; he had more than enough. He was close to God and was nourished by a perfect existence, devoid of deficiency or flaw.

In the second benediction, a new motif wells up. The human being discovers his emptiness, and begins to understand that he has no standing at all. He can be rescued only through God's *hesed*, to which he has no right. Here is an introduction to the prayer of supplication and vigorous entreaty. God is mighty and omnipotent, whereas man is weak and miserable, incapable of earning his bread and fulfilling his needs. Man flees toward God, seeks protection beneath His wings, and presents before Him his supplication, like a slave or maidservant before a master. Man is ready to entreat and plead for undeserved *hesed* from the All-powerful. "You are mighty forever, O God." The "You" excludes everything. Only *You* are high; not *I*: "Who is like You, Master of mightiness." In the first benediction man is aware of his greatness and singularity—he was created in the Divine image, and therefore can approach God; the second benediction expresses man's self-abnegation, his feeling of weakness and his recognition of his own nothingness.

The third benediction commands both the person who believes in his worth and importance and the one who negates his own self to offer up their entire being to God. When man appears before the great God, the God of *hesed*, he is joyful and happy. When he encounters the mighty God, he is filled with dread. When he praises the awesomeness of God, he is prepared to surrender everything to Him.

Prayer and Life

Prayer is not a specific service confined to the cultic realm. The domains of life are intermingled. The service of God is perpetual, without cessation. You can find no action, from the most intimate area to public and national activity, on which the cult does not impress its stamp. Halakhah, which requires a particular form of life consecrated to the one goal of fulfilling God's will, penetrated with its glowing lamp into the hidden places of concrete human existence, physical and spiritual, omitting nothing, oblivious to nothing. Worship must be total and complete, without defect or flaw: "Walk before Me and be perfect" (Gen. 17:1). Worship begins with physiological functions like nutrition and copulation, with the intimate feelings of the individual, with love of parents, and then moves through all of man's public manifestations, his conduct in every nook and cranny of reality, culminating in connections to friends and companions, in business dealings, in professional work that serves society, in the manufacture of economic-industrial products, in social and national initiatives, in political sovereignty. In short, the human being serves God from the fundaments of his vital, instinctual existence to the realms of cultural creativity. Halakhah is concerned with each and every stage of life and leaves its distinctive marks on all of them: "Thus one who follows this path is always serving God, even when he is involved in his affairs, even when he engages in intercourse, for his intention, in all matters, is to satisfy his needs so that his body will be whole for the service of God. Even when he sleeps, if he sleeps in order to rest his mind and body to avoid falling ill and being unable to serve God because of his illness, his sleep is then service to God. This is what the Rabbis meant when they said, 'Let all your actions be for the sake of Heaven' (*Avot* 2:11), and Solomon said in his wisdom, 'In all your ways know Him and He will straighten your path' (Proverbs 3:6)" (Rambam, *Hilkhot De'ot* 3:3).

The first stage in the service of the heart is the integration of halakhic-religious value into the human being's life in all areas, from the lowest instinctual level to the apex of spiritual being.[13] Prayer is not merely an additional stage in the worship of the heart, but, as we have stressed, the mirror that reflects the soul of the worshipper who is totally and perpetually committed to God. Prayer is a kind of information center which reports occurrences in the depths of the love-sick soul. Prayer cannot be separated from life. When the source of an image is placed at a distance from the mirror, the reflection disappears. When the service of the heart is absent in human existence, and the human being is driven by hot, undisciplined and undirected instinct, then prayer is nothing but hypocrisy and insolence. O you empty one, what is the point of expressing with your lips feelings that you never felt, thoughts that never occupied you, borrowed moods and counterfeit experiences? "And to the wicked He said: what is it to you to speak of My laws" (Ps. 50:16). Prayer was established to correspond to the sacrifice of man to God. However, one does not approach Him suddenly according to man's caprice. One does not knock on the royal portals without an invitation. But this invitation is extended to him not in the synagogue, but in the private and public domains which man inhabits: the bedroom, the restaurant, the factory, the office, the seashore and the club. There the invitation is offered, and there the human being encounters God. One who prays cannot diminish the distance between himself and God through cultic enchantment and ceremony, which are useless in themselves. Man must discover the great privilege of coming before God *outside* the sanctuary, in the struggle of existence. Within its precincts there is no wisdom and calculation; here man is treated on the basis of what he has already prepared in the secular domain. Nothing is added or taken away.

Thus, prayer is intertwined with the purity of life and the sanctity of one's overall existence. Robbery prevents man's prayer from being accepted. Sin separates the praying person from his Creator. Dedication to cheap pleasures tarnishes the image of prayer. This is why, at one time, the Rabbis decreed that seminal emission disqualified prayer, "so that men would not copulate like roosters" (*Berakhot* 22a). R. Sa'adyah Gaon devoted a chapter to the laws of prayer, which revolves around one principle: clean hands and pure heart.[14] Prayer, for Sa'adyah, is identical with repentance. Washing one's hands before prayer, omission of which disqualifies prayer according to Rambam,[15] symbolizes the purification of soiled hands from the filth of iniquity and oppression. Hazal command: extend righteousness and charity to the poor before you engage in supplication before God.

This element is known to us from the days of the prophets. Historians err in describing the attitude of the Israelite prophets towards the Temple cult. Under the influence of ancient Christian tradition, which was anti-Judaic and thoroughly detested the Temple, the secular historians state that the prophets negated the institution of sacrifices and the priestly office. The prophets, they say, wished to abrogate ceremonial religiosity *in toto*. These assumptions are based on falsehood and hatred of Israel, rooted in early Christianity. The prophets never fought against the institution of sacrifice in itself, and never intended to strip Judaism of the forms of the Temple cult. Jeremiah, who chastised Israel so much for the proliferation of sacrifices, mourned the destruction of the Temple for many days. In Lamentations, he emphasizes strenuously that the abrogation of sacrifice and festival was an extremely tragic event. Isaiah, who shouted, "For what purpose is the multitude of your sacrifices, says God. I am sated with the burnt offerings of rams, and the suet of fattened animals, and the blood of bullocks and sheep and goats I did not desire" (Isaiah 1:11), prophesied the day when the Temple will stand at the head of all mountains and when offerings will be brought to God (see chapters 2 and 66). No prophet ever rose up against the Temple, Heaven forbid, but rather against a certain spirit among those who made pilgrimages to the Temple. For them, the sanctuary was separated from real life as a special locus for the presence of God, where man appears from time to time before his heavenly Father, there to discharge his oaths and obligations.

The prophets protested against the view that man's world is divided into two domains, the secular and the sacred, and that, within the former, man is free to behave as he desires, without subjecting himself to the yoke of commandment and duty. They protested against the human being who wanted God not to intervene in his private affairs and public conduct. They protested against the view that it is only in the second domain (the sacred) that man must serve God, and that as long as one discharges one's cultic obligations, all is well. The prophets did not tolerate the outlook which says that God requires only one region to be consecrated to His Name, only one region in which man is to unburden himself of the yoke of his many calculations and consecrate himself to the single purpose of worshipping God in holiness. They protested against discontinuity between the secular and sacred domains. They opposed the strange leap from the secular to the sacred, from the defiled to the pure. Against all these phenomena the prophets remonstrated, as well as against the occluded heart that howls sublime utterances and the personality that is insolent outside the Temple, but genuflects and abases itself within its precincts. Any disjunction of the self, any hypocrisy connected with such two-faced conduct, aroused the prophets' abhorrence and revulsion. Worship in the Temple and worship of the heart are both rooted in man's existence as a singular being endowed with identity and continuity. Both prayer and sacrifice are retrospective. The praying person pauses for a moment in his hurried life and looks back at what has been done; if what was done is dishonest and impure, the prayer is an abomination.

Prayer and the Gesture of Surrender

The prayer of the Patriarchs is disclosed to us against this sort of spiritual background. Abraham, the first to discover the constancy of man's service to God, offered the morning service (*shaharit*), but he was occupied with the worship of God day and night:[16] whether sitting at the entrance to his tent at noon or looking up at the blue, star-seeded sky, raising his eyes to wondrous heights as he sought the way up to God; while engaged in dealings with others, in speaking and acting. Prayer began early in the morning, when the universe glistened in the dew of dawn and the rays of the sun. This prayer did not end with the heat of the day; it expresses the aggregate of his past deeds and served as an impulse towards future elevation.

Jewish thought always understood the act of sacrifice as the surrender of something which man's multifarious biological and imaginative appetites crave. The most satisfactory offering to God is the conquest of one's culturally-conditioned desires if they are opposed to God's will. Halakhah did not prescribe total withdrawal from life or an asceticism of the flesh. On the contrary, Halakhah wants man to enjoy God's world. Nonetheless, it demands that man discipline his instincts and lusts, in all areas and with respect to all his capacities. Man is to sacrifice something of the "first fruits of his land," the "first of his dough," the first of his cattle, the first of his toil. The coveting and impulsive heart at times exerts pressure on him with regard to eating and drinking, with respect to his relations with his wife or fellow men. The first commandment given to man as a test of his moral mettle involved a minor renunciation, withdrawal from eating the fruit of one tree. Likewise, when we sanctify the glorious and awesome Name by accepting His decrees, we consecrate ourselves as sacrificial offerings to Him.

Sacrifice is not identical with annihilation. The Torah was interested in life and repelled by death. The altar is built not at man's grave, but at his cradle. On the eighth day [of life] man is offered to God, the circumcision ritual symbolizing the perpetual offering of the Jew's life. His table, his bed, his place of business, his abode—all become altars upon which man offers himself up daily. Man makes his person holy through daily self-control, by renouncing acts of pleasure and satisfaction, by undertaking preoccupations that cause pain and anguish, in order to attain a moral ideal.

Already our Sages depicted sacrifice as a sudden retreat from the fulfillment of cherished desire just at the moment when it reaches its highest tension. When only one step separates total realization from bitter disappointment, the intoxication of happiness from the pain of disappointment—it is then that withdrawal must come. The true commandment of sacrifice splits the being of the person driven by desire; he must avert his face and control the enormous impulse of his boiling blood. The most sublime sacrifice has been offered. The fire of lust has been consecrated to the fire of the altar. The erotic tremor of the personality infested with burning instinctual passion has been purified and brought up to the locus that is consecrated to God. "The groom yearns for his bride. But when he comes to her, she reports seeing a bloodstain like a mustard seed. He turns away, although no scorpion has stung him; no serpent has bitten him—that is the meaning of the verse, 'hedged with roses'" (*Shir ha-Shirim Rabbah* to Song 7:3).

Realization of the moral imperative does not require sanctions and coercive force; it does not need a breach-proof fence. It is like a hedge of roses that is trampled only by the foot of pride. Extraordinary sensitivity to beauty and refinement is implanted in the human personality and restrains the inclination to trample a row of flowers, though beyond that row desire beckons enchantingly, and eye and heart are seduced by it. This row has been devoted to the altar, and the groom who controls his inclination is simultaneously the priest who brings the offering, the sacrifice itself, and the locus of the offering. Wherever such sacrifice takes place, man is worshipping God. How beautiful is the law that the groom must withdraw after the initial cohabitation of the marriage (*Niddah* 65b); or the stringency which Jewish women have accepted to abstain from intercourse for seven days after any flux (*Niddah* 66a). To separate from the bride of one's youth for a brief period is the most sacred and exalted Jewish worship, which the Creator awaits and responds to with love and satisfaction: "Does God desire thousands of rams, multitudes of unctuous rivers?" (Micah 6:7). Sanctity prevails wherever sexual behavior is "fenced off". Sexual behavior is a paradigm for withdrawal from the orgy of lust in all areas. In his *Mishneh Torah*, Rambam included both food prohibitions and sexual prohibitions in the Book of Holiness (*Sefer ha-Kedushah*). Abstention from the lust for forbidden food also rises to the level of a sacrifice to God. On the one hand, the Torah does not recognize the doctrine of asceticism and scorns monasticism. On the other hand, it demands of man to sanctify desires and to elevate the body as an act of worship, thereby damming the current of lust and disciplining the anarchy which represents neither physiological-biological normality nor spiritual achievement. The offerings of surrender and the conquest of inclination constitute a substitute for the great and awesome sacrifice that man is obligated to bring: his fully saturated vitality.

Abraham renounced many things. He rejected the instincts that impelled him to rebellion, he continued to wait for his relationship to be fulfilled in spite of the smug mocking that jeered at him and his obsacle-strewn way of life. He triumphed: "You are holy and Your Name is holy." Before You human prominence must bend, You shake the foundations of the world. And yet, "the holy praise You each day." Reality is sanctified through the self-sacrifice of man, as he is offered up on the altar before God.

Prayer, Absolute Dependence and Tahanun

Prayer is an act expressing total dependence, a prostration in absolute surrender. This act, which, as noted above, bursts forth in the second benediction, brings the praying individual to offer sacrifice—the sacrifice of self through self-discipline, the sacrifice of independence through absolute surrender. Man is disappointed, fate is cruel, life is tainted and ugly and amounts to nothing; wealth, power, and wisdom are naught. There is no refuge for a finite being writhing between being and nothingness; only God can help and rescue. Without Him, rescue is impossible, without Him all is in vain: "All turn to You, to give their nourishment in time. You give them and they glean; You open Your hand and they are filled with good. You hide Your face and they are confused; You gather in their breath and they die, returning to their dust" (Ps. 104:27-29). An irreversible dependency binds everything to the Master of everything, He who nourishes and sustains everything, the one to Whom all raise their eyes, glean from His Hand and anticipate His Mercy. To Him all commit their souls and offer up all they have.

"Do not make your prayer rote, but a plea for mercy and an entreaty before God" (*Avot* 2:13). Pray like a pauper pleading and asking for his needs: "Entreaties speaks the impoverished" (Prov. 18:23). Do not approach God confidently and sedately. Every human being is in need of mercy. Even the fortunate cannot trust in his success. Prosperity is not everlasting. God humbles the proud and raises the humble, relents from evil and at times withdraws benefits.[17] The formula of the abbreviated prayer (Mishnah *Berakhot* 4:4, a short prayer which was recommended by R. Joshua for pressing circumstances) refers to the "multiplicity of needs and the limitation of understanding." It is impossible for man to comprehend his needs and formulate them by means of a lucid prayer. His mouth is inarticulate, his tongue falters. He requires Divine assistance not only for his sustenance but also in order to recognize his deficiencies and to arrange his words: "O God, open my lips and let my mouth utter Your praise," says the praying person when he begins the *Amidah*: that is, it is impossible for me to open my lips and articulate the words. He stands confused before the mighty God. At the conclusion of the prayer, he takes three steps backwards, as one parting from his master. The person who has completed the *Amidah* "falls on his face" in supplication [and recites the *Tahanun* prayer].

This institution of *Tahanun* or *nefilat appayim* stresses the annihilation of man's being. Man lowers himself to the dust and negates his existence. The words of supplication spoken during *nefilat appayim* highlight the tragic character of the pleader: "God, do not rebuke me in Your anger..." (Ps. 6:2). From this plea emerge all the terrors of the miserable and unfortunate person, who bears in his bosom perpetual grief and disgrace. The one who supplicates regrets his sins and calls for help. This formula of entreaty laden with the pain of shame is especially prominent at the moment of *vidduy*, confession. The practice of many communities to recite the *vidduy* (confession) before *nefilat appayim* is not without point. The essence of confession is the demolition of pride and arrogance, leading to a catharsis of the soul that lifts its eyes from the depths of filth.

Centrality of Petition

When we examine the formulation of the benedictions we note that those who arranged the prayer extended the petitions while keeping the celebratory elements (*rinnah*) brief. Entreaty is the back bone of *avodah she-ba-lev*. One who prays on a weekday and omits one of the nineteen blessings does not fulfill his obligation because he does not enumerate properly the needs of the individual and the needs of the community. One who mistakenly recited the weekday prayer on Shabbat has fulfilled the obligation of prayer *be-di-avad,* that is, after the fact, so long as he made some mention of Shabbat.

Even the prayers specified for Shabbat and Yom Tov are not devoid of expressions signifying petition and supplication. To be sure, "Shabbat and Yom Tov are not days to cry out,"[18] yet we plead to Him to purify our hearts, sanctify us through our performance of *mitzvot* and study of Torah, and bestow upon us true goodness, the joy of salvation and of a full respite undiluted by grief. The *musaf*, or "additional," prayer is an outpouring of the heart over Israel's exile from its land and an appeal to God for speedy redemption. A mute sadness suffuses the text of *mippenei hatta'enu* ("Because of our sins") in the Yom Tov *musaf*. There is no prayer without petition and supplication. Halakhah opposed all those outlooks which derive from pantheistic mysticism and which aim to excise entreaty from prayer and to establish worship exclusively on an aesthetic-ecstatic basis of the hymn.

Even though, as noted, prayer requires praise and thanksgiving, nonetheless the vigor and power of prayer derive from petition. Halakhah is interested in psychosomatic man, in his concrete corporeality. It is displeased by the ecstatic separation of soul from body during prayer. The aim of worship of the heart is the offering of sacrifice through the total surrender of body and soul to God. Moreover, Halakhah observes scrupulously the principle of exotericism. The community as a whole cannot escape the bonds of corporeality and its petty needs. Any attempt to require all members of the community to achieve such liberation entails greater loss than benefit. Halakhah is concerned with human beings who dwell in darkness and shadow, who struggle for their bread. Such people are enclosed within their four cubits of distasteful, ridiculous desire. It is such confounded stammerers that Halakhah taught to pray, and into whose mouths it inserted a clear formula. The common man is commanded to offer prayers for the sick in his household, the wine that has turned to vinegar, the crop that has failed. The hymn, embroidered with aesthetic experience is confined to the private domain of the elite. It is pleasing only to mystics, who are characteristically anti-social. Their mode of existence is esoteric; they are spiritually fastidious. Halakhah cannot be confined within the domain of the spiritual nobility. Only petition can bring prayer to the public domain.

So, too, did the greatest figures of the nation prefer entreaty to song. Abraham stood before God in prayer for the people of Sodom. Israel cried out to God in Egypt and at the Red Sea. Moses petitioned God to sweeten the waters of Marah. At Sinai he confronted God over the forgiving of sin; at Hatzerot, he prayed for the healing of Miriam; on the plains of Moab he pleaded with God to enter the promised land. Prayerful supplication and the outcry of the needy burst forth from the Book of Psalms. It is because human outcry predominates over song and praise in this book that it is called *Tehillim* rather than *tehillot:* the latter would ordinarily refer to the plural of *tehillah* (praise) and imply that the theme of the book is praise; the former is not the customary plural, and therefore does not carry the exclusive connotation of praise. Hezekiah, in his illness, turned his face to the wall and prayed (Isaiah 38); Daniel, Esther, Ezra, Nehemiah, lifted their eyes and pleaded with God in their trouble and suffering. It is the hounded and entrapped creature, the tormented being, who cries out to God. Such a prayer is described by Solomon at the inauguration of the Temple: "And You will turn to the prayer of Your servant and to his supplication... When Your people Israel are smitten before a foe... they will pray and plead to You in this house... When the heaven is shut and there is no rain because they sinned unto You, they will pray in this place... When there is a famine or pestilence... Every affliction and sickness, every prayer and supplication that any person has among Your people Israel, when each knows what afflicts his heart, he shall spread his hands towards this house" (I Kings 8:28-38). The needs are varied, and in every case supplication is called for.

The *Amidah* is based on these words enunciated by Solomon. The *Amidah* deals with the needs of this world: bodily health, fertility of the earth, sustenance, political needs of the nation in the land, ingathering of the exiles, restoration of judicial autonomy, the perpetuation of Israel's sages, the building of Jerusalem, the restoration of Davidic kingship, and the like form the background of prayer in all its diversity. The very gesture of falling before God and acknowledging His unlimited sovereignty and man's utter impotence, constitutes an act of sacrifice. Service of the heart is expressed in the middle benedictions.

Need for Praise and Thanksgiving

Nevertheless, as already noted, it is impossible to recite the middle benedictions without the first three. Let me bring out this point by means of an example: "He who goes in a place of wild animals or robbers recites an abridged prayer. What is it? R. Eliezer said: Do Your will in heaven above, and give satisfaction to those who fear You below, and do what is good in Your eyes. Blessed are You, O God, who hearkens unto prayer. R. Joshua said: The cry of Your people Israel—quickly do their petition... Others said: The needs of Your people are many and their intelligence is limited. May it be Your will to give each according to his needs and his deficiency..." (*Berakhot* 29b). This *baraita* deals with a strange problem. According to the Halakhah, the abridged prayer does not fulfill a person's obligation to pray; legally, it does not come under the category of prayer at all. In that case, why did the Rabbis attribute significance to the exact formula of this benediction? Let each person devise his own formula! This *baraita* articulates the idea we just expressed. If the praying individual is unable to present before God the entire order of prayer in its authentic form—to arrange God's praise and beg leave to approach Him boldly, to mention the merits of the Patriarchs and God's graciously attending to the deficiencies of every creature—then he is not permitted to petition for his needs. Egoistic supplication outside the framework of the prayer-formula instituted by the members of the Great Assembly is forbidden. For this reason R. Eliezer prohibited any request. He allowed himself only an eschatological prayer: "Do Your will in Heaven above; do what is good in Your eyes." R. Eliezer prohibits even an entreaty for the community. R. Joshua holds that the Rabbis were somewhat more lenient and allowed supplication to God for the nation in general, but not for individualized needs. Others devised a specific formula, which attests to man's poverty of mind and expresses confidence in God's graciousness, following which it would be permissible to petition for fulfillment of the needs of individuals, but not to detail them.

Prayer as Accepted Sacrifice

The last three benedictions do not constitute a distinct unit. Indeed, when we study them carefully we encounter a mixture of petition and thanksgiving. *Retzeh* ("look with favor upon") and *Sim Shalom* ("grant peace") express supplication. *Modim* is thanksgiving. The Tosafists already perceived the dual motif in the text of the last part of the *Amidah*.[19] *Retzeh* is perhaps the central benediction in the text of *avodah she-ba-lev*. The Mishnah states that the priests in the Temple said this benediction after the offering of the blood of the daily offering (the *tamid*): "They read the Decalogue, [the three sections of *Shema*], and they blessed the people with three benedictions— *emet ve-yatziv* ("true and established," the text recited in our liturgy following the *Shema*), *avodah* (a benediction like *Retzeh*) and *birkat Kohanim* (Mishnah *Tamid* 5:1). The source of this blessing is Lev. 9:22-23, which describes the inauguration of the Tabernacle in the desert: "Aaron lifted up his hands towards the people and blessed them... And Moses and Aaron went out and blessed the people, and the glory of God appeared to all the people." The tannaitic midrash *Torat Kohanim* explains that the first blessing was the priestly benediction (*birkat kohanim*), while the second was a prayer to God to accept the service: They said: "Let the beauty of God be upon us and establish the work of our hands upon us [Ps. 90:17]. And may it be Your will to bestow the *Shekhinah* upon the work of your hands." Thus we find a specific halakhah obligating the priests serving in the Temple to pray at the end of the ritual that the order of worship be accepted as satisfactory. This formula of supplication was transferred from its original place in the Temple ritual to the context of prayer. It is founded on the assumption that the *Amidah*, too, constitutes an act of sacrificial worship, if not in actuality then in one's heart. After the conclusion of the prayer rite one prays that God will be satisfied with the prayer and worship of Israel. The original version of the conclusion is "You alone whom we worship in awe" and the parallel formula is "Who accepts the service of His people Israel with mercy." After the destruction of the Temple this formula was exchanged for a new one, which expresses the national vision and yearning for the restoration of the *Shekhinah* (Divine Presence) to Zion.

What indeed is the essence of this prayer, which the Torah commanded at the time when the Temple stood and human beings offered sacrifice? As noted, the entreaty revolves around the idea of sacrifice. God demands human sacrifice, absolute self-surrender to God. However, God, in His mercy, substituted the flesh and blood of an animal for the action that claims the human body. Yet the spiritual act remains the same. As the smoke of the altar ascends, the human being rises, in his entire being, totally offered to God. Sacrifice and self-binding are here fulfilled. God inhales the odor of fat and blood—not the animal's fat and blood but the person's! Therefore the priests, at the conclusion of the sacrifice pray that God be satisfied with the human sacrifice and accept it, as He accepted the sacrifice of Isaac, even though in actual fact the ram was offered in his stead.

The Tosafists give an interesting explanation of the Talmudic statement by R. Giddel in the name of Rav: "The altar is erected and the angel Michael offers sacrifice upon it" (*Menahot* 110a). Tosafot added: "There is a dispute among the *midrashim*. Some say that he offers up lambs of fire, and that is what is referred to in the *Amidah*, in the blessing of *avodah* as the "burnt offerings of Israel and their prayers." But some say that it refers to the previous phrase, i.e. "restore the cult to Your house and the burnt offerings of Israel."

According to the first interpretation, the phrase *ve-ishei Yisrael* (the burnt offerings of Israel) does not refer to the physical fire on the altar but to a celestial, transcendent offering, and the sacrifice is the soul, the individual personal being of man. This sacrifice continues to exist today; it did not come to an end with the cessation of the daily offerings. The phrase *ve-ishei Yisrael* is connected to the following word *u-tefillatam* (their prayer) [which would mean, "accept with love the burnt offerings of Israel and their prayers. . .] The worshipful entreaty persists today as in days of yore. Nothing has changed with the destruction of the Temple and the cessation of literal sacrifice. Now too we sacrifice to God—that great and awesome offering in which man overcomes his being by ascending to the transcendent metaphysical altar. When a Jew says *Retzeh* he does not refer to the satisfaction of needs and the fulfillment of the desires about which he poured out his heart in the middle, petitionary section. For this he has already prayed in the previous benediction, *Shema Kolenu* ("Hear our voice"). When he reaches *Retzeh* these "petty" matters no longer concern him. His soul is bound up in a great, profound, world-embracing request. He asks God to accept the great sacrifice he has just offered, to accept his being that is returned to God, cleaving unto the Infinite and connecting itself to the Divine throne. God is "satisfied" with this offering. He receives it and restores it to the one who has offered it. The praying individual annuls himself in order to acquire himself. From his prayer man emerges firm, elevated and sublime, having found his redemption in self-loss and self-recovery.

Structure of the Last Three Benedictions

The order of the last three benedictions is the reverse of the opening three. First comes the *Retzeh* blessing which is bound up with sacrifice, as in the third of the opening benedictions, the *kedushat Ha-Shem*. The blessing concerning sacrifice takes precedence over all other aspects of prayer, for a simple reason. The idea of sacrifice is the most puzzling. The question it poses—how can prayer exist in the face of an awesome God, separate from the world, negating all worlds—is a most serious one. The answer, that the essence of prayer at this stage is manifested through man's annihilation in transcendent-metaphysical infinity, that everything belongs to God, is an opaque riddle. We do not comprehend the mystery of sacrifice-prayer, and the idea of restoration is also opaque and not understood—it is beyond human intellectual powers. The problem—how can man appear before God and how can one imagine standing before Him—remains in full force. Therefore, from the outset, we are compelled to say about the whole subject of prayer that it is miraculous from beginning to end. The arrangers of prayer always placed the most difficult element first. They moved from the more difficult to the easier. Therefore we open the last unit of the *Amidah* with a plea for the fulfillment of the sublime, awesome vision—the binding of man and his demise together with his return to existence and being.

Hoda'ah (thanksgiving) corresponds to *Gevurot*. As in *Gevurot*, the sense of dependency is revealed in this benediction. The human being, sensible of God's omnipotence, on the one hand, and his human misery and frailty, on the other hand, lifts his eyes to God's mercy and providence. From this blessing of gratitude, like that of *Gevurot*, emerges the sense of absolute dependence. Man, finding himself in distress, calls out to and thanks God. The praying individual has first fulfilled (in *kedushat Ha-Shem*) the most important action in the framework of *avodah she-ba-lev*—that of consecration and self-surrender.

Following the acceptance of his request that his sacrifice be accepted, man thanks God for its fulfillment. He adopts the optimistic position that God has hearkened to his prayer. As God has accepted his great sacrifice, surely, his prayer shall emerge into the light. Man is grateful for the past and also for the future. He engages in thanksgiving and prayer, although the future is still wrapped in its mysterious secrecy. In this blessing, the experience of trust reaches its climax. Vision becomes reality, desire becomes fact, prayer becomes complete certitude; this trust is founded primarily on the absolute morality of Divine activity. As He is infinitely merciful, His goodness is unconditional and unlimited; why should He not come to the aid of an abashed, downtrodden person who reaches out to Him? God's might appears in His mercy. The benediction contains the phrases "[You who are] good, for Your mercies are not exhausted, and [You who are] merciful, for Your *hesed* has not ended— we have ever hoped unto You"; "Blessed Art Thou, Lord, Whose Name is good and for Whom gratitude is fitting."

At the end of the prayer we return to the benediction of *Avot*, the initial approach of the worshipper to God. Great is his trust in the everlasting God. God's mercies have no bounds. His goodness flows through all being. Indeed, God dwells with him. He is omnipresent; we recognize that reality is enveloped with infinity. What is existence, if not the light of the infinite Face! What is wealth, if not the gift of God! What do we want? What do we crave? What do we seek?—only cleaving unto Him. The God of Abraham, the God of the universe who relates to being from both without and within, He is the God of peace and blessing and good.

Man begins: "Bestow peace, good and blessing, life and grace, *hesed* and mercy upon us and all Israel Your people." In other words, after all the transformations and oscillations from love and mercy to the experience of dread and human helplessness, after man comes crashing down from the heights of yearning and aspiration to the depths of confusion and terror, after self-negation and self-recovery, after the sacrifice, the binding and the offering on the altar, and after the return to existence—comes again the delightful, joyous and confident experience: God appears as a safe haven and secure abode. The praying individual lies down in green pastures [Ps. 23:2], cleansing himself before God like a son before his father. His tempest-tossed, riven soul finds happiness and serenity, all fear being forgotten. Dread has disappeared; the awesome mystery is past. In their place is a welling up of joy and a yearning for communion with the source of being. Man does not flee from God, but rather races towards Him and resides in the bosom of the *Shekhinah*. All is blanketed in the serenity of peace and quiet. Over all, there flows the blessing of the Infinite; the *hesed* of God descends "like the dew on Mount Hermon" (Ps. 133:3). The word is illuminated with the precious light that flows from the Infinite.

1. For sources, see R. Y. Perla's commentary to *Sefer ha-Mitzvot le-R. Sa'adyah Gaon*, Positive Commandment 2.

2. *Guide* III:51.

3. Notes to Rambam's *Sefer ha-Mitzvot*, Positive Commandment 5.

4. *Hil. Tefillah* 4:1. See *Hiddushei R. Hayyim ha-Levi ad. loc.*: "There are two types of intention with respect to prayer: one is the intention relating to the meaning of the words, which is grounded in the principle of intention; the second is that he should intend that He is standing before God."

5. Whether *kavvanah* is necessary for the performance of the *mitzvah* to be valid is a matter of dispute. According to many Talmudic sages and decisors, intention must accompany, and is a necessary condition of fulfillment. According to many other decisors, however, lack of intention does not prevent fulfillment of the *mitzvah*. But even if intention is required, it is distinct from the action itself. See *Rosh Ha-Shanah* 28b; *Berakhot* 13a; *Pesahim* 114b and parallels, and *Milhamot Ha-Shem* and *Sefer ha-Maor* to *Rosh Ha-Shanah*.

6. Note, however, that Moses saw and spoke with God not out of terror and trembling but in serenity. See Rambam *ibid.*

7. *Berakhot* (26b), cited by Rambam, *Hil. Tefillah* 1:5; *Hil. Melakhim* 9:1.

8. See *Berakhot* 21a and Tosafot *s.v. R. Yohanan* and Rif, *Berakhot* ch. 4; Rambam, *Hil. Tefillah* 1:6. See also *Orah Hayyim* 107:4 ("Would that one have proper intention for the three daily prayers...").

9. *Guide* I:54: "It has been explained to you that the attributes and ways are one, and they are the actions that come from Him in the world..." See also I:59.

10. Ramban, Commentary to Leviticus 1:9.

11. See the story about the death of R. Meir's two sons *Yalkut Shimoni*, Proverbs section 964.

12. Ramban, Leviticus 1:9: "The sprinkling of the blood on the altar corresponds to his own blood, so that a person may consider in doing any of this, that he has sinned against his God, body and soul, and that it is his blood that ought to be spilled and his body that ought to be immolated, were it not for the Creator's *hesed*, who took from him a substitute."

13. *Guide* III:51.

14. *Emunot ve-De'ot* 5:6.

15. *Hil. Tefillah* 4:2.

16. *Guide* III:51: "For of these four, that is the Patriarchs and Moses, it is explained that they unified their thoughts with the divine while occupied with human activities and acquiring possessions."

17. Rambam, *Hil. Yesodei ha-Torah* 10:4.

18. This is the formula utilized in praying for the sick on Shabbat and Yom Tov, when explicit petition is barred (based on *Shabbat* 12a).

19. Tosafot, *Berakhot* 34a, s.v. *al yish'al adam*.

❧ Index of Topics and Names

❧ Index of Biblical and Rabbinic Sources